The Birth of the British Empire

The Birth of The British Empire

A Basic History

D.W.J. Allen

Copyright © 2022 Daniel Allen All rights reserved

No part of this book may be reproduced, or stored in a retrieval system, or transmitted in any form or by any means, electronic, mechanical, photocopying, recording, or otherwise, without express written permission of the publisher.

ISBN- 9798416676537

Cover design by: Daniel Allen using Amazon Cover Creator.

Front cover image of Jamestown by istock.com/visionsofmaine.

Back cover image of The Battle of Quiberon Bay- 1759.

Image taken from an 1896 edition of the Navy & Army Illustrated.

Accessed via istock.com/Cannasue.

Contents

Acknowledgements	vi
About this book	vii
A quick note on language	x
Introduction: The Birth of the British Empire	1
Chapter 1: Why the Empire Matters	3
Chapter 2: Imperialism	21
Chapter 3: What was the British Empire?	31
Chapter 4: Pirates	41
Chapter 5: Trade	59
Chapter 6: Colonies in the Americas	73
Chapter 7: England's Empire in Britain	91
Chapter 8: War	105
Chapter 9: The Global Situation	123
You made it!	139
About the author	141

Acknowledgements

As with many books of this scale, this is a work of synthesis. That means I've worked more with modern history books than contemporary sources. With that in mind, I must give my heartfelt thanks to the numerous historians whose work I have referenced in this text.

Of course, even with all the fantastic works that have gone before me, I couldn't have written this alone. For that reason, I am enormously grateful to all of the friends and family who gave me their feedback and advice ever since this book was nothing more than a series of blog posts.

About this book

This book is a little different to traditional history books. This is because its main goal is to make history more accessible. I want to introduce people to ideas they may not have read about before in a way that is quick, easy to read, and simple to understand. There are several ways that I've attempted to do this.

For a start, this book is shorter and focuses on a much narrower topic than most history books aimed at a general reader. I don't want it to be a time-consuming read, quite the opposite. I hope it will help many of you quickly expand your knowledge of this important period of history and inspire you to pursue further study.

I also include many quick explanations of people, groups, and events that may initially seem irrelevant to the book's subject. When picking up a book on the early British Empire, who would expect to end up reading a short biography of Vladimir Lenin or an overview of the Second Sino-Japanese War? Not many of you, I suspect. There is, however, method to my madness.

One of the major barriers to a budding student or enthusiast of history is that there is so much of it. Because of how closely linked everything is, a reader often requires some existing knowledge already to fully appreciate whatever they are reading and make their own judgements on it. I hope that these quick explanations go some way in helping you to overcome this issue. If you are already confident in your knowledge of these topics, feel free to skip over them, but I hope that all of you will find at least a few helpful.

Another barrier to students of history can be the type of language used. Many history books use complicated language that makes them inaccessible. In some cases, this is unavoidable. Discussing complicated topics may well need complicated words. However, I have tried to keep my language as simple as possible. I want anyone to be able to access this work, regardless of their reading level or existing knowledge.

Finally, as I've said, my aim for this book is to introduce you to new topics, ideas, and different ways of thinking. It's not to argue the case for my own personal interpretation of history. Sometimes, I may give you my opinion, but often, I prefer to provide you with the debate and let you decide for yourself which side you think is right. As much as possible, I try to be balanced when approaching the topics in this book and give multiple points of view a fair chance.

Of course, you don't need to read the entire book from cover to cover if you don't want to. I designed it to be read that way, but it could work just as well if you use it as a reference book to dip in and out of when you what to learn about a particular topic. Ultimately, this book is for you to help you develop your knowledge of and approach to history. You can read it however suits you.

This book started as a series of blog posts on my website, dallenhistory.com, although I have added substantial amounts of new content here that has not been seen before. In the future, I hope to write more books like this one. As such, I have a small request for you. I am very aware that I'm trying something a little bit different with the format of this book. It is certainly new to me, and I suspect it will be new to you also. If, while reading it, you find things that you like and feel work particularly well, then it would mean a great deal to me if you let me know! Likewise, if there are ways that you think I could improve this series, then I would also love to hear from you.

Last but not least, I hope you enjoy reading this book as much as I enjoyed writing it.

Contact info:

Twitter: @dallen_history

Instagram: @dallenhistory

Facebook: @dallenhistory

A quick note on language

You may notice that sometimes I refer to 'Britain' and the 'British Empire', while other times I refer to 'England' and the 'English Empire'. This is because 'Britain' as a state didn't really exist until the early eighteenth century, so it is sometimes more appropriate for me to talk about England. That being said, events in England obviously contributed to the later British Empire. Therefore, I try to use whichever term I find most appropriate for my point. If, for example, I am discussing Oliver Cromwell fighting the Scottish or Irish, it feels more appropriate to discuss the 'English' rather than the 'British' Empire.

Introduction: The Birth of the British Empire

Most people in Britain today are familiar with the British Empire. How could they not be? It's everywhere. In books, in newspapers, on our televisions, and on social media. We can't escape it, and we shouldn't try to.

I have been interested in the empire for as long as I can remember. I grew up reading stories and watching films in which scarlet-coated soldiers fought across the globe, and British gentlemen were found sipping tea in exotic hotels. As I grew older, I started to think about the empire in more detail. I explored the dark side of imperialism to go with the stories of heroism and bravery I had consumed as a child, and I realised that I'd never stopped to consider how Britain acquired its empire. In my childish mind, the empire seemed to spring into life fully formed. The factories of Victorian England appeared and loaded shining steamships with goods to be sold all around the world. With that in mind, when I decided to start this series, my first challenge was to explore how the people of Britain came together and formed a global empire. As such, this book covers topics ranging from the medieval period to the early eighteenth century.

This was not an easy task as it is a vast topic that combines many different areas of specialism. Medieval historians, experts on the Tudor and Stuart periods, historians of slavery and war, those that study business and trade, or culture and everyday life, everyone has a part to play, and this book is indebted to the research of a great many outstanding historians.

I don't claim that you'll find all the answers within these pages. That after reading this book, you'll have discovered the hidden truth of how and why Britain transformed itself into an empire that, for better or for worse, has had an enormous impact on the world. However, I hope you will find the knowledge to help you decide how you think the empire was born, why you think the people of Britain spread across the globe, and how you think they managed it.

The first three chapters of this book are quite theoretical and maybe at times a bit abstract. We will start by discussing why the British Empire still matters today, then look at what an empire is, and finally, where the British Empire fits into the broad category of 'empires' by asking ourselves, 'what was it?'. With this done, we can move on to the book's primary purpose. As such, the rest of the text analyses and explains important themes surrounding the start of the British Empire.

First, I'll cover pirates and trade before discussing why Britain established colonies in the Americas, then analyse the extent to which the British Isles themselves were an empire. Our penultimate chapter examines the role of wars in the rise of the British Empire, while the final chapter draws everything together and looks at Britain's place in the world by the early eighteenth century.

Chapter 1: Why the Empire Matters

Section 1: Introduction and Explanations

The first thing we need to discuss is why this was a book worth writing and why it's worth your time reading. If you've picked it up, I assume you already have some ideas on why this book may be interesting or valuable. If, however, you're still a bit unsure, this chapter can hopefully reassure you that you aren't wasting your time.

There are three explanations to go with this chapter. The first discusses the Mughal Empire, which dominated India before the British took over. Given the importance of India to the British Empire, I'm sure it's clear why this is relevant. The second is on the Opium Wars, which defined the British relationship with China in the nineteenth century. If you don't know about these wars, you should read this before the main chapter, as understanding them will be crucial to help you understand the global legacy of the empire.

The final explanation is about Operation Ichigo, a significant event in China during the Second World War. This might seem odd at first, but there is a good reason for it. In this chapter, I discuss the argument that Britain's actions during the Second World War helped justify its empire, a relatively common defence. Understanding Operation Ichigo and the war in East Asia more generally is an excellent way of putting Britain's actions during the war into context.

What was the Mughal Empire?

The Mughal Empire was formed by Muslim invaders who conquered Northern India in the sixteenth century. At its peak, it controlled almost the entire Indian subcontinent. It had a vast military, a massive population, and a considerable proportion of the world's wealth. It was one of the strongest empires on Earth at this time.

Mughal Emperors also launched many grand construction projects. The most famous was the Taj Mahal, which Shah Jahān built as a mausoleum for his wife.

The Mughals were heavily involved in trade with Europeans. At first, they held much of the power in the relationship. Europeans had to gain the permission of the Mughal Emperor to trade and construct their factories, and early English attempts at using force were unsuccessful.

In the late seventeenth century, however, the unity of the Mughal Empire began to crack as internal revolts ravaged it. Into the eighteenth century, external invasions added to this pressure as the British forcibly extracted more concessions from the empire. This included the right to collect taxes and, effectively, the power to rule the valuable province of Bengal. Economically, the Mughals failed to keep up with European agriculture and industry. Eventually, Mughal control disintegrated across the empire until the British took over formal rule of India in the nineteenth century.[1]

What were the Opium Wars?

The Opium Wars were two conflicts in which the British and other Europeans forced China to open up to global trade.

The British had for a long time been smuggling opium into China, which left many Chinese people addicted to the drug and destabilised the economy. In response, officials representing the Qing Dynasty (then rulers of China) took British citizens hostage and forced them to hand over their opium stocks. Outraged by this, the British Government retaliated with overwhelming force. They launched a massive land and sea offensive and seized multiple Chinese cities.

In 1842, the First Opium War ended with the extremely harsh 'Treaty of Nanjing'. This treaty forced the Chinese to open several ports up to European trade, pay an enormous sum of money in compensation, and cover the costs of the war. Furthermore, the treaty capped the tax rate that the Chinese could charge on imports at a minuscule 5% and gave British citizens in China immunity from Chinese law. No wonder this is often considered the first of the 'Unequal Treaties'.

After all this, the Chinese were, unsurprisingly, still reluctant to trade. In 1856 the British and French allied to launch another assault on China. This time, the victory was even more complete and tragic. The European troops even captured the capital city Peking (modern Beijing).

In retaliation for the mistreatment of some captured prisoners of war and despite French protestations, British troops systematically destroyed the beautiful Summer Palace of the Chinese Emperor. Following this, they forced China to completely open up to European trade and pay another considerable fee.[2]

What was Operation Ichigo?

Operation Ichigo was a massive offensive launched against China by the Japanese in 1944. It was the last and the largest of the major Japanese offensives of the Second World War. They deployed over 500,000 soldiers and aimed to destroy the army of the Chinese Kuomintang (KMT) government and demolish American airfields in China.

The Japanese planned Ichigo thoroughly. They had been stockpiling ammunition for two years, and when they launched the offensive, their troops were supported by tanks, artillery, and airpower. In contrast, Chinese forces were very poorly equipped.

For that reason, the early stages of Ichigo were a massive success for Japan. Estimates suggest that they killed forty Chinese for every Japanese soldier lost. There were genuine fears that the KMT government would fall, and the situation became so desperate that 100,000 students joined the Chinese army.

As well as the differences in armaments, many other factors weakened the Chinese position. For a start, their British and American allies let them down by refusing to listen to warnings about Ichigo. They even took many of the best Chinese troops to support their campaign in Burma.

There were also internal issues and infighting within the KMT itself. Its leader, Chiang Kai-Shek, refused to reinforce one general because he wasn't sure of the man's personal loyalty to him. At the same time, he wasted troops laying siege to the communists, refusing to redeploy them even as the situation grew more and more desperate.

Eventually, the Japanese overextended their supply lines. Their troops began to starve, and the offensive ground to a halt. They hadn't met all their aims. The Americans could still bomb Japan, and the KMT still existed, but it paid a heavy price. Of the one million KMT troops who fought in this campaign, between 500,000 and 600,000 of them died, leaving the government severely weakened.³

Section 2: Why does the British Empire still matter?

Why is it worth discussing the British Empire? It's gone, isn't it? What's the point in bringing up bad memories? Well, there are many arguments for why studying history is valuable. We can learn from past mistakes and understand the present. Or, maybe we study history for simple interest and enjoyment, or even as an intellectual exercise.[4] But there is a much more tangible and immediate reason to explore the British Empire. To put it simply, the British Empire never really went away. There is a wealth of evidence showing the legacy of the empire in Britain and around the world. Beyond this, although the empire may have ended in the sense that Britain no longer directly rules countries like India and Jamaica, in a broader sense, it still exists.

Effects on Britain

One noticeable impact that the empire had on Britain that is still highly relevant today is racial conflict and prejudice. Many believe that the Transatlantic Slave Trade (the shipping of enslaved people from Africa to North America) led to modern racist ideas on the superiority of white people over black.[5] Given Britain's heavy involvement in the trade, this is one of the dubious gifts left to us by the empire.

However, the empire was also highly influential in developing modern Britain's diverse and multicultural population. Many immigrants came to Britain as citizens of the empire to help or even fight for the country that had colonised them.[6]

This combination of racist ideologies and a diverse population has led to many conflicts and a great deal of pain faced by many people of colour.[7] It is a clear legacy left to us by our imperial past and one that shows no sign of disappearing any time soon.

The empire has also left its mark upon Britain in many ways beyond racism. The rhetoric used by politicians and the way they discuss events around the globe are rooted in Britain's imperial past.[8] Likewise, in his excellent book *Empireland*, Sathnam Sanghera demonstrated a wide variety of impacts that the empire still has upon Britain, including eating habits, the contents of museums, and even country houses funded by the slave trade.[9] The empire's effects on Britain are all around us.

Global politics and conflicts

The British Empire has contributed to many tense disputes and struggling regions in the world today. Even as its empire crumbled, Britain desperately attempted to cling to power and undermined stability in many places.

Iraq and Iran

In 1942, during the height of the Second World War, the British and the Soviets made plans to guarantee that they could access Iranian infrastructure following the war. This left the Iranian people feeling abused and exploited.[10] As late as 1950, the British also maintained a firm grip on Iraq.[11] It seems probable that resentment of this heavy-handed treatment has contributed to recent tensions between this region and the West.

India and Pakistan

The tensions between India and Pakistan can be traced back to the British Empire's time in the region. The Japanese assault on Britain's empire in East Asia forced Britain's political leaders to promise independence to India.[12] The problem was, once it became clear that Britain wouldn't be able to maintain the dominance they wanted after independence, they did not stay around to ensure a peaceful and stable transfer of power.[13] Soon after the end of the Second World War, Lord Mountbatten, the last Viceroy governing British India, convinced his superiors in London that if Britain did not withdraw quickly, they would be drawn into a chaotic conflict between different Indian factions.[14] The British rapidly split their possessions into two states: India and the Islamic state of Pakistan.[15] This decision forced millions of people to emigrate considerable distances to reach the appropriate country for them. Over a million people died.[16]

Hong Kong

Britain governed Hong Kong for over a century, during which it became a hub of capitalism in East Asia.[17] At the end of the twentieth century, they returned Hong Kong to the governance of the People's Republic of China.[18] China's recent history has been turbulent, to say the least. For well over a century, foreign powers and corrupt officials abused China and its people.[19] Most notably, during the Opium Wars, the British and other European powers violently forced China to open its borders to trade.[20] This has led to China's wariness of foreign involvement in its country and the adoption of a political system of 'socialism with Chinese characteristics.'[21] A hub of capitalism re-joining a socialist government was never likely to go smoothly, so the recent conflicts here should come as no surprise.

Africa

Africa, too, is still struggling with the legacy of British rule. The colonial era created new countries with many internal divisions. Colonial powers such as the British inflamed and manipulated these divisions, leading to many conflicts between ethnic groups.[22] The consequences of this mishandling were civil war, the decline of the rule of law, and starvation.[23] As a result, parts of Africa, even today, remain somewhat reliant on foreign support.[24]

The benefits of the empire

It would be unfair of me to only focus on the harmful effects of the empire; it certainly did some good. There is, of course, the favoured argument of imperial apologists that the empire brought railways worldwide. It may be a cliché and overused defence, but it remains true that the empire did help improve infrastructure in its colonies, in some cases at least.[25] Likewise, the British Empire did try to eradicate many practices that we today would find disgusting, such as widow burning, cannibalism and (eventually) slavery.[26] It was also a major driver of globalisation and the movement of people around the globe, helping to create a diverse and multicultural world.[27] Therefore, the British Empire was also responsible for many features of the world that we may find favourable.

The trouble with blame

We must also be careful when assigning too much blame to the British Empire. Jeremy Black argues that we must remember Britain was rarely invading self-governing democracies. Often, it was invading other empires.[28] This fact may change how we view some of the empire's more aggressive actions early in its history. However, it hardly serves as an excuse for its sinister activities after the Second World War.

Black also believes that some people blame the empire for problems that would have occurred anyway due to population change and globalisation.[29] He is not wrong. An example of this is Shashi Tharoor's *What the British did to India*.[30] It is an interesting analysis of Britain's damaging effect on India that certainly helps dismiss the more basic arguments that Britain was good for India's development. However, Tharoor does tend to blame Britain for all the economic decline in India, which was not the case.[31] The Mughal Empire was already declining before the British became heavily involved there. Without this decline, it's entirely possible that Britain would have never gained such a strong foothold in India.[32]

Finally, on the issue of Ethiopia requesting the return of items from British Museums, Black points out that Ethiopia had stolen some of these from other African nations during its own time as an empire.[33] This complicates the issue of returning artefacts somewhat.

It is clear then that we must be careful not to just present the British Empire as entirely 'evil'; things were a little more complicated than that.[34]

Was Britain the world's champion?

Going even further than Black, Niall Ferguson argues that the British Empire's darker aspects were necessary to create the modern world.[35] He also claims that the British Empire was ultimately justified because the British sacrificed their empire to defeat the Nazis and the Japanese.[36] Is Ferguson right? Was the British Empire the unsung hero that made the difficult choices no one else would and saved us from an infinitely greater evil? Of course not. There are several problems with this argument.

Britain was one among many

First, let's not overstate Britain's role in winning the Second World War. Britain did, of course, play a significant part in the Allied war effort. It was one of the major powers. But that's also the problem. It was *one* of the major powers, not *the* major power. To focus too much on Britain's contribution risks diminishing the catastrophic loss of life faced by the people of the Soviet Union and China (roughly 20 million and 14 million people, respectively).[37] The Allies even bullied the Chinese KMT government into sending troops they absolutely could not spare to fight the Japanese in British Burma.[38] This act contributed to the enormous defeat that they suffered during Operation Ichigo.[39]

Credit where credit is due

Another problem with Ferguson's argument is the implication that we should give the British Empire credit for the actions of the people it had colonised. Should we not instead be praising and thanking the citizens of the Empire for being willing to fight for a power that had consistently abused them and hardly been thankful for their valiant contributions in the First World War?[40]

How can you sacrifice something you still tried desperately to keep?

Finally, and perhaps most problematically of all, is the idea that the British Empire committed some heroic self-sacrifice. This argument just doesn't hold up under scrutiny. The British government never believed they genuinely had to relinquish their empire, even if they gave up formal rule. For centuries the empire had been about more than just traditional control, and British ideas of imperialism were no different during and after the Second World War.[41]

British plans for the post-war world always included the idea that English-speaking people would at least temporarily continue to be dominant.[42] Even President Roosevelt agreed that the so-called 'Great Powers' would need to be in control.[43] The British believed they could continue dominating their former colonies using the Commonwealth.[44] We have already seen that they went to great lengths to defend their interests in the Middle East and continued to assert their economic dominance following the war. Despite rising nationalism and other setbacks in their colonies, they truly believed they could recover.[45]

The problems with defending the empire

I hope I have shown you that we need to be careful of some of the classic defences of the British Empire. I agree that we shouldn't simply dismiss it as evil; things were more complicated than they may first appear. However, the defences of the empire are often far too Eurocentric and can add even more pain to Britain's former imperial subjects.

The Empire lives on

B. R. Tomlinson argued that the British Empire ceased to exist as an 'economic phenomenon' between 1967 and 1973 when the Pound's value dropped and Britain joined the European Economic Community.[46] This may seem surprisingly recent, but I actually don't believe this argument goes far enough. In many ways, the British Empire still lives on around us.

Globalisation and the West

I'm a big fan of globalisation, and multiple historians have pointed out Britain's role in bringing free trade worldwide.[47] The problem is that the version of globalisation that we currently have doesn't live up to its ideal form. In a perfectly globalised world, everyone would have equal opportunities for free movement and economic development. That's not what we have. This is because not everyone entered the period of globalisation as equals. During the Cold War, world leaders feared that Western nations' already powerful financial positions would mean that imperialism would continue to thrive.[48] This fear has been proven right. Globalisation has meant that former colonies remain dependent on their imperial overlords.[49]

Ferguson has tried to dismiss the idea that British rule economically hurt its colonies by showing that the economic gulf between Britain and Zambia has widened since Britain gave up formal control of the country.[50] This is both unsurprising and in no way a valid defence of the empire. Considering the various negative legacies left by the British and the inherently unfair world order they helped to create, of course its former colonies continue to struggle.

When will the Empire be gone?

This fact, above all else, makes it clear why we still need to study the British Empire. It still exists. Britain still reaps the benefits from the global conditions that its empire created, which means it still has a privileged position in the world order.[51] No wonder politicians speak as if Britain is still an imperial power; in many ways, it remains one. Informal imperialism is still well and truly alive, and until Britain's former colonies have the chance to compete fairly on the global stage, so is the British Empire.

---

[1] Sources:
Darwin, J., *After Tamerlane: The rise and fall of global empires, 1400-2000*, Penguin edition (London: Penguin, 2008).
Darwin, J., *Unfinished empire: The global expansion of Britain*, Penguin edition (London: Penguin, 2013).
Fisher, M. H., *A short history of the Mughal Empire*, (London: I.B. Tauris, 2016).
Frankopan, P., *The silk roads: A new history of the world*, paperback edition (London: Bloomsbury, 2016).
Hunt, T., *Ten cities that made an empire*, Penguin edition (London: Penguin, 2015).
Marshall, P. J., 'The English in Asia to 1700', in *The Oxford History of the British Empire: Volume 1, the origins of the empire, British overseas enterprise to the close of the seventeenth century*, ed. by N. Canny, 5 vols (Oxford: Oxford University Press, 1998), pp. 264-285.
Schama, S., *A history of Britain: The British Wars 1603-1776*, Kindle edition (London: Bodley Head, 2009).

[2] Sources:
Bickers, R., *The scramble for China: Foreign devils in the Qing Empire, 1832-1914* (London: Penguin, 2012).
Darwin, J., *Unfinished empire: The global expansion of Britain*, Penguin edition (London: Penguin, 2013).

Fenby, J., *The Penguin history of modern China: The fall and rise of a great power, 1850 to the present*, 3rd edition (London: penguin, 2019).
Hunt, T., *Ten cities that made an empire*, Penguin edition (London: Penguin, 2015).
Schama, S., *A history of Britain: The fate of the empire, 1776-2000*, Kindle edition (London: The Bodley Head, 2009).

[3] Sources:
Fenby, J., *The Penguin history of modern China: The fall and rise of a great power, 1850 to the present*, 3rd edition (London: penguin, 2019).
Hsi-sheng Ch'I, 'The military dimension, 1942-1945', in *China's bitter victory: The war with Japan, 1937-1945*, ed. by J. C. Hsiung and S. I. Levine, new edition (Abingdon: Routledge, 2015), pp. 157-184.
Mitter, R., *China's war with Japan, 1937-1945: the struggle for survival* (London: Penguin, 2014).
T'ien-wei Wu, 'Contending political forces during the war of resistance', in *China's bitter victory: The war with Japan, 1937-1945*, ed. by J. C. Hsiung and S. I. Levine, new edition (Abingdon: Routledge, 2015), pp. 51-78.
van de Ven, H. J., *War and nationalism in China: 1925-1945*, (Abingdon: RoutledgeCurzon, 2003).

[4] J. H. Arnold, *History: A very short introduction* (New York: Oxford University Press, 2000).
[5] H. Arendt, *The origins of totalitarianism*, Penguin Classics edition (London: Penguin, 2017), pp. 230-31; S. Sanghera, *Empireland: How imperialism has shaped modern Britain* (London: Viking, 2021), pp. 142-164: A. Jackson, *The British Empire: A very short introduction* (Oxford: Oxford University Press, 2013), p. 116.
[6] Akala, *Natives: Race and class in the ruins of empire*, paperback edition (London: Two Roads, 2019), pp. 6-7; Eddo-Lodge, R. *Why I'm no longer talking to white people about race*, expanded edition (London: Bloomsbury, 2018), pp. 10-13, 22-23; Sanghera, *Empireland*, pp. 69-84.
[7] Akala, *Natives*; Eddo-Lodge, *No longer talking*; Sanghera, *Empireland*, pp. 69-84, 142-164; you can also look at countless examples on social media or in the news, such as the recent abuse of footballers after Euro 2020.
[8] J. Paxman, *Empire*, Penguin edition (London: Penguin, 2012), pp. 4, 277; Sanghera, *Empireland*, pp. 105-09.
[9] Sanghera, *Empireland*.
[10] P. Frankopan, *The silk roads: A new history of the world*, paperback edition (London: Bloomsbury, 2016), pp. 399-401.
[11] Frankopan, *The silk roads*, pp. 399-405.

[12] J. Darwin, *Unfinished empire: The global expansion of Britain*, Penguin edition (London: Penguin, 2013), p. 345.
[13] Darwin, *Unfinished empire*, p. 339-40.
[14] J. M. Brown, 'India', in *The Oxford History of the British Empire: Volume 4, the Twentieth Century*, ed. by J. Brown and Wm. Roger Louis, 5 vols (Oxford: Oxford University Press, 1999), pp. 421-446, (p. 437).
[15] M. Wood, *The story of India*, Kindle edition (London: BBC Books, 2008), chapter 6.
[16] Brown, 'India' p. 437; Darwin, *Unfinished empire*, pp. 348-49.
[17] T. Hunt, *Ten cities that made an empire*, Penguin edition (London: Penguin, 2015), pp. 258-59.
[18] Hunt, *Ten cities*, pp. 1-3.
[19] R. Bickers, *The scramble for China: Foreign devils in the Qing Empire, 1832-1914* (London: Penguin, 2012); R. Bickers, *Out of China: How the Chinese ended the era of Western domination* (London: Penguin, 2018); J. Fenby, *The Penguin history of modern China: The fall and rise of a great power, 1850 to the present*, 3rd edition (London: penguin, 2019).
[20] Bickers, *Scramble for China*, pp. 80-81, 149; Fenby, Penguin modern China, pp. 9-10, 22-23; Hunt, Ten cities, pp. 235-247.
[21] J. Black, *Imperial legacies: The British Empire across the world* (New York: Encounter Books, 2019), pp. 90-91; Xi Jinping, *The governance of China: Volume 1*, 2nd edition (Beijing: Foreign Language Press, 2018), pp. 3-33.
[22] Jackson, *The British Empire*, pp. 109-112.
[23] T. Falola, 'West Africa', in *The Oxford History of the British Empire: Volume 4, the Twentieth Century*, ed. by J. Brown and Wm. Roger Louis, 5 vols (Oxford: Oxford University Press, 1999), pp. 515-529, (pp. 528-29).
[24] Frankopan, NSR, pp. 114-115. J. Lonsdale, 'East Africa', in *The Oxford History of the British Empire: Volume 4, the Twentieth Century*, ed. by J. Brown and Wm. Roger Louis, 5 vols (Oxford: Oxford University Press, 1999), pp. 530-543, (pp. 542-43).
[25] N. Ferguson, *Empire: How Britain made the modern world*, Penguin edition (London: Penguin, 2004); pp. 169-170; Paxman, *Empire*, pp. 150-53; S. Tharoor, *Inglorious empire: What the British did to India*, Penguin edition (London: Penguin, 2017), pp. 176-82.
[26] Paxman, *Empire*, pp. 202-05; R. J. Blyth, 'Britain, the Royal Navy and the suppression of the slave trades in the nineteenth century', in *Representing slavery: Art, artefacts and archives in the collections of the National Maritime Museum*, ed. by D. Hamilton and R. J. Blyth (Aldershot: Lund Humphries in association with the National Maritime Museum, 2007), pp. 76-91; Jackson, *The British Empire*, pp. 122-23.
[27] Ferguson, *Empire*, pp. xiii, xxii; Paxman, *Empire*, pp. 8-9.
[28] Black, *Imperial legacies*, pp. 11-12.

[29] Black, *Imperial legacies*, p. 12.
[30] Black, *Imperial legacies*, pp. 26-27.
[31] Tharoor, *Inglorious empire*.
[32] J. Darwin, *After Tamerlane: The rise and fall of global empires, 1400-2000*, Penguin edition (London: Penguin, 2008), pp. 82-86, 143-44; Darwin, *Unfinished empire*, pp. 50, 77; Hunt, *Ten cities*, p. 190.
[33] Black, *Imperial legacies*, p. 38.
[34] Jackson, *The British Empire*, pp. 120-21.
[35] Ferguson, *Empire*, p. xviii.
[36] Ferguson, *Empire*, p. 363.
[37] R. Mitter, *China's war with Japan, 1937-1945: the struggle for survival* (London: Penguin, 2014), p. 6.
[38] Mitter, *China's war*, pp. 249-62, 302-04, 330-36.
[39] Mitter, *China's war*, pp. 321-23, 346, 352.
[40] Eddo-Lodge, *No longer talking*, pp. 10-23; Sanghera, *Empireland*, pp. 65-84.
[41] J. Gallagher, and R. Robinson, 'The imperialism of free trade', *The Economic History Review*, 2nd ser., 6.1 (1953), 1-15; Grady, J. and Grocott, C., *The continuing imperialism of free trade: developments, trends and the role of supranational agents* (Abingdon: Routledge, 2019). This is an excellent edited collection covering such ideas.
[42] M. Mazower, *Governing the world: the history of an idea* (London: Penguin, 2013), p. 194.
[43] Mazower, *Governing the world*, p. 196.
[44] Darwin, *Unfinished empire*, pp. 342-43.
[45] Darwin, *Unfinished empire*, pp. 352-55.
[46] B. R. Tomlinson, 'Imperialism and after: The economy of the Empire on the periphery', in *The Oxford History of the British Empire: Volume 4, the Twentieth Century*, ed. by J. Brown and Wm. Roger Louis, 5 vols (Oxford: Oxford University Press, 1999), pp. 357-377, (p. 358).
[47] Black, *Imperial legacies*, pp. 8-9; Darwin, *Unfinished Empire*, pp. 179-80; Gallagher and Robinson, 'Imperialism of free trade', 1-15; Ferguson, *Empire*, pp. 365-68; S. Schama, *A history of Britain: The fate of the empire, 1776-2000*, Kindle edition (London: The Bodley Head, 2009), chapters 5 and 6.
[48] J. Dinkel, '"Third World begins to flex its muscles": The Non-Aligned Movement and the North-South conflict during the 1970s', in *Neutrality and neutralism in the global Cold War: Between or within the blocs?*, ed. by S. Bott et al, (London: Routledge, 2015), pp. 108-23 (pp. 113-114).
[49] Tharoor, *Inglorious empire*, p. 236; V. Prashad, *The darker nations: A people's history of the Third World*, (New York: The New Press, 2007), p. 34.
[50] Ferguson, *Empire*, p. 368.

[51] Jackson, *The British Empire*, p. 114, UN security Council and diplomacy.

Chapter 2: Imperialism

Section 1: Introduction and explanations

This chapter is all about understanding imperialism. While I am sure you have probably heard the term before picking up this book, have you ever stopped to consider what 'imperialism' actually is? What makes something become an empire? After reading this chapter, you will hopefully understand some key ideas surrounding this divisive topic.

Before we get to that, however, I have a couple of quick explanations for you. Marxism is a crucial part of the debate surrounding empires and imperialism, so I think it will be helpful if we quickly review the broader Marxist theory of history first. After that, we're going to look at the life of Lenin, the founder of the Soviet Union. Before becoming Russia's leader, Lenin wrote a very influential book on his theory of imperialism. I highly recommend that those who don't know much about him give this a read. It should be helpful to remember that behind all of these big theories are people, each with their own lives and experiences.

What is the Marxist theory of history?

The traditional Marxist theory of history is based on Karl Marx's argument that the working class would eventually rise and topple capitalism. The theory argues that history is progressive, and society gradually develops through multiple stages before, finally, communism becomes supreme. Many historians, especially in the Soviet Union, have used Marx's theory to understand the past. However, others have criticised it for not giving enough value to the actions of individuals and for, focussing too much on Europe and not being globally applicable. Likewise, the general prosperity of Western countries following the Second World War seemed to contradict Marx's argument that capitalism would lead to poverty, which damaged the global relevance of Marxism.

Many well-known historians such as E. P. Thompson, Christopher Hill, and Eric Hobsbawm tried to overcome these issues and breathed new life into Marxist history. They, along with many others, created various interpretations of Marxist history. Lots of these more recent interpretations focused more on historical context and the individual circumstances of people and groups than traditional Marxists, who focused mainly on economics. For example, the school of subaltern studies analysed the uniqueness of different colonised people. At the same time, in his *The making of the English working class*, Thompson emphasised the distinctiveness of the British working-class experience.

Over the twentieth century, socialism struggled, and capitalism appeared to have won, becoming the dominant global system. The use of the Marxist theory of history declined and is now less widespread than in the mid-twentieth century. However, the popularity of Marxist history has been rising again in recent years, as some writers have used it to study US global dominance and the links between imperialism and globalisation.[1]

Who was Lenin?

Vladimir Ilyich Lenin was born in 1870 into a relatively privileged Russian family. His father started his life firmly in the lower classes but rose through the ranks of the Russian civil service and provided a comfortable life for his family.

When Lenin was 17, his older brother was executed for being involved in a plot to assassinate the Tsar (the Russian king/emperor). This event likely radicalised Lenin. Following his brother's death, he gave up hobbies such as music and chess to focus solely on the revolutionary cause. He read various German and Russian revolutionary texts, including Karl Marx's *Communist Manifesto*.

Lenin worked as a revolutionary for many years, participating in student riots during his time at the University of Kazan and eventually fleeing the authorities and going into hiding. The First World War provided an excellent opportunity for him, but he was trapped in Zurich for much of the conflict, along with many other leading revolutionaries. During this time, he wrote his important text, *Imperialism: The highest stage of capitalism*. This outlined his theory on the evils of capitalist expansion, which he believed had caused the war, and the need for worldwide revolution.

In 1917, food riots started by the starving people of Russia soon turned to violence and, eventually, mutiny. The Russian Monarchy fell. Lenin was still in Zurich when this happened. Once they heard the news, Lenin and his comrades rushed back to Russia as quickly as possible. Elections were held, in which Lenin's Bolshevik party performed relatively poorly, but this didn't stop him. Driven by his ideology and belief that the Bolsheviks represented the best choice for the people of Russia, Lenin destroyed the provisional government and seized control of the country.

He led Russia, which became the Soviet Union, until his death in 1924. Despite his relatively short time in charge of the country, Lenin's ideas were crucial for its following leaders. From Stalin and Khrushchev to Mikhail Gorbachev, every single one tried to portray themselves as Lenin's true successor.[2]

Section 2: Understanding Empires and Imperialism

Imperialism is a vague and difficult term to grasp. Many different people have many different opinions on what makes an empire and what it means to practice imperialism.[3] This often leads to confusion and to the disagreements we see over how imperial legacies should be treated today. However, I believe that one thing the major theories on imperialism all have in common, whether they look at 'formal' or 'informal' empires, is power.[4] Therefore, I argue that the best way to understand imperialism is to view it as the use of any form of power to dominate others. Power is key in the forms that imperialism takes and the theories explaining how and why it happens.

Forms of Imperialism

To begin, we should address some of the different forms that imperialism can take.

Formal

Power is quite obviously central to what we can call 'formal' imperialism. This is often the form of imperialism we associate with the Roman Empire, which is reflected in the language that the Romans themselves used to discuss their empire. Although 'imperialism' is a modern term introduced in the nineteenth century, it has an ancient ancestor. The Latin word *Imperium* initially meant the power to give orders and the geographical area in which these orders would be followed.[5] Later, it came to mean, more simply, the area under Roman authority.[6]

Beyond language, Donald Baranowski believes that the ancient historian Polybius' conception of Roman power was strikingly similar to the modern theory of imperialism, where a state exerts military, political or economic dominance over another, weaker state.[7] This suggests that the Roman elite managed their empire by issuing formal commands and governing foreign territories. In this form of imperialism, it is quite easy to see the central role of power.

Informal

Power still plays a considerable part even in theories focussing on 'informal' empire. In their influential article 'The Imperialism of Free Trade', John Gallagher and Ronald Robinson argued that it is wrong to only think of imperialism being present when we see signs of formal control.[8] Instead, they believed that informal means of control were just as important markers of imperialism.[9]

According to them, what Britain really wanted from its empire was the right to trade and to be able to sell their manufactured goods. Where possible, they did this without formally invading a country. The British only invaded when they felt they had to in order to secure their trade.[10] Instead, they preferred indirect means of control, such as using the reliance of people in southern Africa on British ports to dominate the region.[11] Although this form of control is very different from the physical occupation exerted in a more formal type of imperialism, this still ultimately shows one nation using its power to dominate others for its own benefit.

Motivations for Imperialism

From the evidence we have seen, it's quite clear that although imperialism may take different forms, it is always an expression of power. The same is true when we look at what the motivations for imperialism may have been.

Hobson and Marxism

In the early twentieth century, J. A. Hobson published his *Imperialism: A Study*. In this, he argued that the imperialism of his time resulted from rising nationalism and competition between rival empires. He believed that the increasing competition over land led states to become more and more militaristic.[12]

A variety of Marxist thinkers, including Vladimir Lenin, later took up and expanded upon this theory. Lenin believed that imperialism was the final stage of capitalism, resulting from 'monopoly capitalism'. He argued that imperialism occurred when firms became extremely powerful, dominating their markets and accelerating the race to capture raw materials, which included new lands and colonies.[13] This is a view shared by many other Marxist writers, who all saw imperialism as something that grew from capitalism at the end of the nineteenth and beginning of the twentieth centuries.[14] Plainly, power is central to this understanding of imperialism. In this context, it is the power not just to dominate other people and states but to exploit them and the land on which they live.

Schumpeter

Lenin's understanding of imperialism is quite narrow, focussing as it does on a very specific period. Joseph Schumpeter created a broader theory explaining the motives for imperialism. He did not think that imperialism was something unique to capitalism. Instead, he saw it as a form of continuous military expansion.[15] In his mind, states were expanding and being aggressive for no reason other than simply being victorious.[16] In this theory, power remains vital, but there is a twist. States are not using their power to gain any particular benefit. Instead, they are using their power for its own sake.

Hardt and Negri

Michael Hardt and Antonio Negri published their book *Empire* after the fall of the Soviet Union. In it, they argue that it is now possible for an 'empire' to exist without the practice of 'imperialism'. According to them, imperialism used to consist of nation states pushing beyond their borders, whereas now an empire exists that is not tied to any single nation. Thanks to globalisation, an abstract empire has formed, composed of a variety of national and international bodies.[17]

Although many believe that the current world order is an age of American imperialism, Hardt and Negri disagree. They argue that the USA symbolises the new world order, not because of its privileged position but because its constitution is based on the distribution of power through networks.[18]

Put simply, the new global 'empire' is power in its purest sense. It is no longer the result of one state targeting others but is an expression of global power with no single leader. It is the combined might of many different people and groups and spans the globe.

What this means for studying the British Empire

Understanding some fundamental theories and debates about imperialism and empires is crucial to understanding the British Empire. In the next chapter, we will look at how diverse the empire was and the different ways in which people have approached it. These differences might not have made sense if you weren't aware of how complicated approaches to imperialism and empires can be. However, after reading this chapter, you are well prepared to begin tackling the nuances of the British Empire.

---

[1] Sources:
Bayly, C., 'History and world history', in *A concise companion to history*, ed. by U. Rublack (Oxford: Oxford University Press, 2012), pp. 3-25.
Breisach, E., *Historiography: Ancient, medieval and modern*, 3rd edition (London: University of Chicago Press, 2007).
Burrow, J., *A history of histories*, Penguin edition (London: Penguin, 2009).
Claus, P., and Marriot, J., *History: An introduction to theory, method and practice*, new edition (Abingdon: Routledge, 2013).
Noonan, M., *Marxist theories of imperialism* (London: I.B. Tauris, 2017).
Wang, Q. E., and Iggers, G, G., *Marxist historiographies: A global perspective* (Abingdon: Routledge, 2016).

[2] Sources:
Lenin, V. I., *Imperialism: The highest stage of capitalism*, (London: Penguin, 2010).
Krausz, T., *Reconstructing Lenin; An intellectual biography*, tr. B. Bethlenfalvy (New York: Monthly Review Press, 2015).
Mazower, M., *Dark continent: Europe's twentieth century*, Penguin edition (London: Penguin, 1999).
Roberts, J. M., and Westad, O. A., *The Penguin history of the world*, 6th edition (London: Penguin, 2013).
Possony, S. T., *Lenin: The compulsive revolutionary*, new edition (Abingdon: Routledge, 2017).
Swain, G., *A short history of the Russian Revolution*, (London: I. B. Tauris, 2017).
Williams, B., *Lenin: Profiles in power*, new edition (Abingdon: Routledge, 2014).
Wood, A., *The origins of the Russian Revolution, 1861-1917*, e-Library edition (London: Taylor and Francis, 2001).

[3] B. Bush, *Imperialism and postcolonialism* (New York: Routledge, 2014), introduction.
[4] J. M. Mackenzie, 'The significance of the British Empire' in N. Dalziel, *The Penguin Historical Atlas of the British Empire* (London: Penguin, 2006), pp. 8-9, discusses this idea.
[5] M. Beard, *SPQR: A history of Ancient Rome* (London: Profile Books, 2014), p. 196; C. B. Champion, and A. M. Eckstein, 'Introduction: The study of Roman Imperialism', in *Roman Imperialism: Readings and sources*, ed. C. B. Champion, (Oxford: Blackwell, 2004), pp. 1-16, (pp. 1-3).
[6] Beard, *SPQR*, p. 196.
[7] D. Baronowski, *Polybius and Roman Imperialism* (London: Bloomsbury Academic, 2011), pp. 11-13.
[8] J. Gallagher, and R. Robinson, 'The imperialism of free trade', *The Economic History Review*, 2nd ser., 6.1 (1953), 1-15 (pp. 1-4).
[9] Gallagher and Robinson, 'Imperialism of free trade', 1-4.
[10] Gallagher and Robinson, 'Imperialism of free trade', 5-6.
[11] Gallagher and Robinson, 'Imperialism of free trade', 3.
[12] J. A. Hobson, *Imperialism: A study* (New York: Gordon Press, 1975). First published 1902, pp. 9-11.
[13] V. I. Lenin, *Imperialism: The highest stage of capitalism*, (London: Penguin, 2010), pp. 156-63.
[14] Noonan, M., *Marxist theories of imperialism* (London: I.B. Tauris, 2017), chapter 1.
[15] Champion and Eckstein, 'Introduction', p. 2.
[16] J. A. Schumpeter, 'The Sociology of Imperialisms' in *J. A. Schumpeter: The Economics and Sociology of Capitalism*, ed. by R. Swedberg, (Princeton:

Princeton University Press, 1991), pp. 141-219. First published 1918, (p. 143).
[17] M. Hardt and A. Negri, *Empire*, paperback edition (London: Harvard University Press, 2001), preface.
[18] Hardt and Negri, *Empire*.

Chapter 3: What was the British Empire?

Section 1: Introduction and Explanations

Now that we've explored why the British Empire matters and had a look at what an empire is and how imperialism works, we need to look in a bit more detail at the nature of the British Empire. How did it work? What do historians think about it? What did people at the time think about it?

The explanations for this chapter aim to break down one event that it is crucial you know about to understand the British Empire and one equally important group of laws. The event is the Glorious Revolution, and the laws are the Navigation Acts. These will come up again and again in books on the British Empire, especially the early period of the empire. If you don't know about them or want to refresh your memory, here's your chance.

What was the Glorious Revolution?

King James II ruled as an absolutist, meaning he believed he should have the final say on the governance of England. Parliament disliked this and was especially concerned by James' desire to restore Catholicism and force wider religious toleration on the country. Thus, the Dutch Protestant William of Orange, who was married to James' daughter Mary, raised an army and landed in England. He deposed James, and parliament offered him the crown. This event marked a turning point in British history, as parliament's power began to grow and the Monarch's to decline.[1]

What were the Navigation Acts?

The Navigation Acts were a series of laws introduced from 1651 onwards. They created a system of imperial trade that lasted into the nineteenth century. Although these laws changed and adapted over time, their central aim remained the same. This was to ensure that Britain retained control over trade with its colonies. The Acts stated that trade between Europe and British colonies would have to go through British citizens and generate profit for Britain. As a further benefit, they also created an economic network that tied the empire together and maintained a high level of merchant shipping, which helped the Royal Navy in times of war.[2]

Section 2: What was the British Empire?

In the last chapter, we discovered the wide variety of forms that imperialism can take and that the primary common link between all these forms is the projection of power over others. So, where does the British Empire fit onto the spectrum? Unfortunately, this question has no easy answer. Essentially, the British Empire was a mix of the various forms of empire we've studied. John Mackenzie explained this nicely when he argued that the British Empire was not one single empire but many different empires coinciding.[3] The nature of the British Empire changed both over time and across space.

Today, many people have wildly different opinions on the empire; the same was true throughout its history. There was never a consensus on what it should be and whether it was good or bad. Because of this, we cannot assign any broad label to it beyond the expansion of the power of the British people abroad. However, we can look at all the multiple faces and features of the empire to develop a sophisticated understanding of what was and remains a very complex entity.

Change over time

One straightforward way the empire changed over time was the decreasing role of the royal family in imperial imagery. During the early stages of imperialism, the king was a crucial part of imperial rhetoric. However, by the early eighteenth century, this had started to change, as people began to talk more about 'Britons' and 'Britannia'.[4] As Linda Colley has argued, British people started to define themselves as free Protestants, aligned against the unfree Catholic French.[5]

People in England and the English colonists in America repeatedly tried to limit the power of kings.[6] Events like the Glorious Revolution contributed to a growth in the strength of parliament and the development of laws, legislatures, and written constitutions.[7] These developments meant that across the seventeenth and eighteenth centuries, less attention was paid to royal authority and more to the power of the English and, later, the British people. The monarchy did remain an important symbol, especially in the colonies, but it now did so alongside a much stronger and more confident parliament.[8]

Another topic that shows how the British Empire changed over time is the slave trade. In the early nineteenth century, Britain morphed from a pro-slavery to an aggressively anti-slavery nation.[9] Initially, its success in this was limited, as the ships stationed off the coast of West Africa were too few, too old, and too slow to be particularly effective in chasing down slavers.[10] However, the British sent more ships over time, and the government began to pressure buyers of enslaved people in Brazil and became more directly involved in West African politics. By 1865 the slave trade was effectively defeated.[11]

An even stronger example of how the empire changed over time is the idea that it transitioned from a 'First' to a 'Second' form. The theory goes that the 'First British Empire' was located in the Atlantic region and based on commercial regulations like the Navigation Acts, maintaining closed trade networks between the colonies and Britain.[12] Many see the 'Second British Empire' as a shift towards the East (such as India) and the rise of free trade, partly because of the American Revolution and subsequent suspicion of formal imperialism.[13]

Geographical differences

The British Empire consisted of so many diverse regions that it would be impossible for us to describe any standard control methods across all land under British influence; such common approaches did not exist.[14] In the American and West Indian colonies, power was shared between an elected assembly with control over taxation and appointed officials from Britain.[15] Things were entirely different in India, where the country was primarily run like a dictatorship by a tiny number of officials.[16] Local factors, such as the agency of the East India Company as opposed to the British state, were always incredibly important.[17] Therefore, it is clear that when we think of the British Empire, we have to think of various measures of control, and multiple different types of imperialism, rather than just one.

A wide variety of modern opinions

Some people still think positively of the empire. In the 1970s, Jan Morris described themself as 'a child of my times' and admitted feeling sympathy for the imperialists, despite accepting that they were often selfish or 'brutal'.[18] Into the twenty-first century, for Niall Ferguson, the defining features of the empire were its large size and role in shaping the modern world.[19] Such views seem to support the idea that the British Empire made the people of Britain feel 'special'.[20]

However, many people take the opposite view and point to the numerous crimes of the empire. For instance, Shashi Tharoor argues that far from helping India to develop and industrialise, the British Empire suppressed indigenous Indian manufacturing.[21] Sathnam Sanghera points out that the crimes of the empire have also caused many problems in modern society, such as the resurgence of racism and white supremacy.[22] Elizabeth Thornberry has shown that issues such as translation and the competition for power between traditional African leaders and the imperial government made it very difficult for women in colonial South Africa to get justice for sexual violence.[23] Meanwhile, Elizabeth Kolsky has detailed how a legal quirk meant that Europeans had practical immunity from prosecution in India's interior for a period in the eighteenth century. In theory, judges in Calcutta could have held them to account, but few Indians had the means to pursue this.[24] Although reformers took steps to improve the situation, even in the second half of the nineteenth century, there were still attempts to assert inequality.[25] These are just a few examples of some of the empire's less savoury actions.

There is also diversity in what methods scholars use to approach the British Empire. Traditional studies of the empire like that of J. R. Seeley or J. A. Hobson focussed on political accounts. Today increasing attention is being paid to issues such as race, gender, and identity.[26] This is partly due to the postcolonial movement, which aims to give a voice to those who traditionally have been silenced.[27]

Debates over the empire are nothing new

Throughout its history, there was never any consensus about how the empire should be run and, what it should look like, even whether it should exist. John Darwin has argued that the British Empire was one of 'private enterprise', created and maintained by many individuals, each with their own motives and beliefs.[28] It is unsurprising then that some felt uncomfortable with the idea of a formal empire after the disastrous (for Britain) American Revolution, making them want to focus on free trade.[29]

Liberty was essential in British ideology, and there was genuine concern over whether imperial rule infringed on colonists' rights or whether the perception that it could lead to the moral improvement of the colonised made it worthwhile.[30] Such debates provide a question mark over the claims that the empire was about the rise of the British state as opposed to the British people. The British people sometimes viewed the power of the state with suspicion.[31]

There were also very diverse opinions over how the empire should treat other peoples. J. R. Seeley watched with satisfaction as the numbers of the Maori in New Zealand fell as he believed this to be in Britain's best interests.[32] In total contrast, those who supported the anti-slavery movement pursued inter-racial kinship. This is demonstrated by anti-slavery medallions, one featuring a kneeling enslaved black person with the words 'Am I not a man and a brother?' inscribed upon it and another commemorating the abolition stating 'We are all brethren'.[33] Similarly, in 1844 General Charles Napier criticised the empire, saying that the British had inflicted incredible cruelties upon the people of India in the pursuit of profit.[34] In the twentieth century, the writer George Orwell served in the imperial police in Burma. He saw the suffering inflicted on the Burmese by the empire as part of a broader pattern of global suffering, which included the poor in Britain.[35] Thus, while some claimed the superiority of Britain and Britishness, others were struggling hard to forge international kinship and pointing out the pain the empire caused across the globe.

Knowing all this, how should we approach the British Empire?

Hopefully, I have shown quite how complicated studying the British Empire can be. It never really existed as one coherent, homogeneous political body, and much debate and disagreement surrounded it from the very beginning. This diversity means it can be tough to develop our interpretations and understandings of the empire today. However, it can be done if we are willing to look holistically, paying attention to the various features that made it.

---

[1] Sources:

Kay, R. S., *The Glorious Revolution and the continuity of law* (Washington, D. C.: The Catholic University of America Press, 2014).
Miller, J., *The Glorious Revolution*, 2nd edition (New York: Routledge, 2014).
O'Gorman, F., *The long eighteenth century: British political and social history, 1688-1832*, 2nd edition (London: Bloomsbury, 2016).
Schama, S., *A history of Britain: The British Wars 1603-1776*, Kindle edition (London: Bodley Head, 2009).
Simms, B., *Three victories and a defeat: The rise and fall of the First British Empire, 1714-1783*, Penguin edition (London: Penguin, 2008).
Wilson, M. I., *Happy and glorious: The revolution of 1688* (Stroud: The History Press, 2014).

[2] Sources:

Darwin, J., *Unfinished Empire: The global expansion of Britain*, Penguin edition (London: Penguin, 2013).

Marshall, P. J. 'Introduction' in *The Oxford History of the British Empire: Volume 2, The Eighteenth Century*, ed. by P. J. Marshall, 5 vols (Oxford: Oxford University Press, 1998), pp. 1-26.

Rodger, N. A. M. *The command of the ocean: A naval history of Britain*, new Penguin edition (London: Penguin in association with the National Maritime Museum, 2006).

Sawers, L., 'The Navigation Acts revisited', *The Economic History Review*, n.s., 45.2 (1992), 262-284.

Schama, S., *A history of Britain: The British Wars 1603-1776*, Kindle edition (London: Bodley Head, 2009).

Simms, B., *Three victories and a defeat: The rise and fall of the First British Empire, 1714-1783*, Penguin edition (London: Penguin, 2008).

[3] J. M. Mackenzie, 'The significance of the British Empire' in N. Dalziel, *The Penguin Historical Atlas of the British Empire* (London: Penguin, 2006), pp. 8-9, (p. 8).

[4] I. K. Steele, 'The anointed, the appointed and the elected: governance of the British Empire, 1689-1784', in *The Oxford History of the British Empire: Volume 2, The eighteenth century*, ed. by P. J. Marshall, 5 vols (Oxford: Oxford University Press, 1998), pp. 105-126, (pp. 105-14).

[5] L. Colley, *Britons: Forging the nation, 1707-1837*, revised edition with new introductory essay (New Haven: Yale University Press, 2005), p. 5.

[6] G. Chet, *The colonists' American Revolution: Preserving English liberty, 1607-1783* (Hoboken: Wiley Blackwell, 2020), pp. 64-65.

[7] Chet, *Colonists' American Revolution*, pp. 64-67; F. O'Gorman, *The long eighteenth century: British political and social history, 1688-1832*, second edition (London: Bloomsbury, 2016), p. 43/

[8] O'Gorman, *Long eighteenth century*, p. 43; Steele, 'Anointed, appointed, elected', pp. 114-115.

[9] J. Black, *Imperial legacies: The British Empire across the world* (New York: Encounter Books, 2019), p. 2; S. Sanghera, *Empireland: How imperialism has shaped modern Britain* (London: Viking, 2021), p. 36.

[10] R. J. Blyth, 'Britain, the Royal Navy and the suppression of the slave trades in the nineteenth century', in *Representing slavery: Art, artefacts and archives in the collections of the National Maritime Museum*, ed. by D. Hamilton and R. J. Blyth (Aldershot: Lund Humphries in association with the National Maritime Museum, 2007), pp. 76-91, (p. 79).

[11] Blyth, 'Suppression', p. 84.

[12] P. J. Marshall, 'The First British Empire', in *The Oxford history of the British Empire: Volume 5, historiography*, ed. by R. Winks, 5 vols (Oxford: Oxford University Press, 1999), pp. 43-53, (pp. 43-46).

[13] Marshall, 'First British Empire', p. 51; J. Morris, *Heaven's command: An imperial progress*, new paperback edition, (London: Faber and Faber, 2012), pp. 24-25.

[14] J. Darwin, *Unfinished empire: The global expansion of Britain*, Penguin edition (London: Penguin, 2013), p. 169.
[15] J. R. Ward, 'The British West Indies in the age of abolition, 1748-1815', in *The Oxford History of the British Empire: Volume 2, The eighteenth century*, ed. by P. J. Marshall, 5 vols (Oxford: Oxford University Press, 1998), pp. 415-439, (p. 434).
[16] L. James, *The rise and fall of the British Empire*, new edition (London: Abacus, 1998), pp. 219-20.
[17] C. A. Bayly, 'The Second British Empire', in *The Oxford history of the British Empire: Volume V, historiography*, ed. by. R. W. Winks, 5 vols (Oxford: Oxford University Press, 1999), pp. 54-71, (pp. 65-66).
18 Morris, *Heaven's command*, p. 10.
[19] N. Ferguson, *Empire: How Britain made the modern world*, Penguin edition (London: Penguin, 2004), pp. xi, xxvi-xxviii.
[20] J. Paxman, *Empire*, Penguin edition (London: Penguin, 2012), p. 5, discusses this idea.
[21] S. Tharoor, *Inglorious empire: What the British did to India*, Penguin edition (London: Penguin, 2017), pp. 5-9, 27-34.
[22] Sanghera, *Empireland*, p. 164.
[23] E. Thornberry, *Colonizing consent: Rape and governance in South Africa's Eastern Cape* (Cambridge: Cambridge University Press, 2018), pp. 298-99.
[24] E. Kolsky, 'Codification and the rule of colonial difference: Criminal procedure in British India', *Law and History Review*, 23 (2005), 631- 683, (p. 641).
[25] Kolsky, 'Codification', 641, 650-51, 658-60.
[26] J. Peacey, 'Introduction', in *Making the British Empire*, ed. by Jason Peacey (Manchester: Manchester University Press, 2020).
[27] R. J. C. Young, *Postcolonialism: A very short introduction* (New York: Oxford University Press, 2003), pp. 1-2.
[28] Darwin, *Unfinished empire*, p. xi.
[29] Morris, *Heaven's command*, pp. 24-25.
[30] Bayly, 'Second British Empire', p. 54; James, *Rise and fall*, p. xiv.
[31] J. R. Seeley, *The expansion of England: Two courses of lectures*, (Cambridge: Cambridge University Press, 2010). First published 1883, p. 43, argued that the empire was also about the expansion of the English State.
[32] Seeley, *Expansion of England*, p. 47.
[33] 'Medal commemorating the abolition of the slave trade' (1807) https://collections.rmg.co.uk/collections/objects/255125.html; 'Slave Emancipation Society medallion', (c.1787-1790) https://collections.rmg.co.uk/collections/objects/254428.html.
[34] Sanghera, *Empireland*, p. 164.
[35] S. Schama, *A history of Britain: The fate of the empire*, 1776-2000, Kindle edition (London: The Bodley Head, 2009), Chapter 8.

Chapter 4: Pirates

Section 1: Introduction and Explanations

Now it's time to get to the real purpose of this book and start looking at how the British Empire began. In its early stages, the empire was quite informal; colonies and conquering came later. Therefore, in this chapter, we will look at the role of pirates, or more accurately, privateers.

There are a lot of explanations to go with this chapter, and they're all quite important to be able to make sense of what I'm discussing. First up, you'll want to know what privateers are, so if you don't, then make sure to read that one. After that, I'll discuss Oliver Cromwell and Queen Elizabeth I. They're famous figures, so you may already know who they are. However, if you don't, it would be helpful for you to know a bit about two of the most important English rulers in the period covered by this book.

The next two explanations are also about important figures of this age, Sir Francis Drake and Sir John Hawkins. They were two of the earliest and most successful English privateers. Of course, pirates and privateers needed someone to steal from, so we'll also discuss the Spanish Empire. Finally, all the money flowing into England had to be spent on something, so the last explanation is about the Levant Company.

Who were Privateers?

Privateers were pirates who were legitimised by a king, queen, or some other form of authority. In return for their legitimacy, they gave this authority figure a share of the profits they made while plundering. Rulers saw this as a cheap way of waging war and continued to use privateers even as official navies developed.

The term was created in the seventeenth century, although in practice, we can see privateering in action much earlier. It was rife in Elizabethan England, where Queen Elizabeth I permitted English seamen to attack Spanish ships.

In theory, privateering was only legal during times of war, but there were many grey areas. Influential investors (including the queen) made significant sums of money, and another state could always legitimise privateers if their own was at peace. It was often hard to distinguish privateering from regular illegal piracy, and the Spanish (who were constant victims of privateering) saw them as criminals.[1]

Who was Oliver Cromwell?

Oliver Cromwell was born into the English minor gentry and was a member of parliament during the English Civil War. We know little about his early life. However, we know that he became a passionate Puritan Christian and rose through the ranks to become a significant leader of parliament's New Model Army during the Civil War. This is despite having had no previous military experience.

After parliament's victory and the execution of King Charles I, he went on to subjugate the Scots and the Irish. Many historians emphasise the brutality of his actions in Ireland in particular; some have even argued that Cromwell aimed to eradicate Catholicism in the country.

Later, he became disillusioned with the actions of the parliament he had spent his life serving. Therefore, in 1653 he rallied the army and dissolved parliament, becoming Lord Protector of England and ruling until his death. However, after he died, much of his work was undone. Struggling to find a successor, parliament returned the throne to Charles II, son of the executed Charles I. After this, supporters of the royal family started attacking Cromwell's reputation and legacy.[2]

Who was Queen Elizabeth I?

Queen Elizabeth I is often remembered as one of England's greatest and most popular leaders. She stabilised the country after years of religious conflict during the reigns of her father, Henry VIII and siblings, Edward and Mary. Under her rule, English sailors halted the invasion of the Spanish Armada and brought wealth back to the country by pillaging Spain's colonies in the Americas.

Despite the successes of her reign, her early years were filled with sorrow and danger. When she was born, Elizabeth was a massive disappointment to parents who had hoped desperately for a son to provide a secure heir to the throne. Her gender caused her more problems in adulthood when councillors seemed more inclined to defy her because she was a woman. However, Elizabeth refused to be defined by her gender and defied all expectations by never marrying.

After her father and brother died and her sister Mary became queen, Elizabeth came close to being executed. However, Mary's husband, Philip II of Spain, prevented this as he suspected Mary might not live for long and believed that he could work with Elizabeth. Additionally, because of the questionable nature of her parents' marriage (Henry had defied the Pope and divorced his first wife), many in England thought Elizabeth was not even a legitimate heir to the throne.

Despite all these obstacles, Elizabeth ascended to the throne of England in 1558. The country was in a bad place. For a start, it was impoverished. Philip had used England's money to fund his wars, essentially bankrupting it to help Spain. This was one reason why Elizabeth was always willing to back those who had a plan to bring treasure back to her country.

Naturally, she made powerful enemies. Mary had turned England back into a Catholic state after the Protestant rule of her father and brother. Elizabeth reversed this, making the country Protestant again. As a result, the Pope excommunicated her and even tried to have her assassinated. Her willingness to face this was one example of her bravery, which, along with intelligence and charisma, helped to create her reputation as a great ruler.

However, she was certainly not a perfect queen. She was vain, arrogant, and despite outwardly showing confidence, she was often very indecisive. Her government struggled to maintain appropriate taxes and, especially in the later years of her reign, became very inefficient and chaotic. Nevertheless, despite her flaws, the English people greatly missed Elizabeth after her death. Her reputation as a good queen still stands today.[3]

Who was Sir Francis Drake?

Sir Francis Drake is a famous figure in British history and has received enormous attention over the centuries. This fame extends back to his own time when his circumnavigation of the world and the riches he brought back to England from privateering and piracy made him a celebrity and a hero to many in the country.

He is often remembered today for his daring adventures, such as attacking the Spanish fleet harboured in Cadiz or fighting the Spanish Armada. However, Drake's life was darker than these tales of swashbuckling raids on the Spanish may suggest. Although he later allied with runaway enslaved people in the Americas to fight the Spanish, he began his career as a slave trader.[4]

Who was Sir John Hawkins?

Sir John Hawkins was a younger son from a famous family of sailors, desperate to make his name and fortune. Queen Elizabeth I permitted him to conduct a slaving voyage, taking captives on the African coast before selling them in Spanish America. His voyages made tremendous amounts of money, he became a national hero, and the queen knighted him. However, his final voyage was a disaster.

Trading in the Spanish colonies had already upset the Spanish government. They believed that only they had the right to trade with their territories, and they grew even angrier when a hurricane blew Hawkins' small fleet off course to Mexico. Hawkins seized control of a port to repair his ships and secure provisions. Soon after, a Spanish fleet arrived, and a battle ensued from which only two English vessels escaped. One was commanded by Hawkins himself and the other by his cousin, the young Francis Drake.

An enormous amount of money had been invested in the expedition for little return. The largest ship sunk with much of its treasure aboard, and most of the crew were lost. It was a catastrophic failure.

After this disaster (which heightened the already increasing tensions between England and Spain), England and Hawkins turned more and more to piracy. He continued developing new plans for fighting the Spanish at sea, even formulating a daring plan to capture their treasure fleet.[5]

What was the Spanish Empire?

At the end of the fifteenth century, Spain was in a curious place. On the one hand, the Christian kingdoms of Aragon and Castille, now united in marriage, had finally defeated Spain's last Muslim kingdom and unified the country. On the other hand, Spain was very far behind its neighbour Portugal in colonial progress. Therefore, when Christopher Columbus proposed crossing the Atlantic to reach India, Spain's rulers jumped at the chance. Of course, Columbus did not find India, but he did find the Americas.

The Spanish Empire rapidly expanded across this new world. It began in the Caribbean, where Spaniards flocked to the islands hoping to find gold and eradicated most of the indigenous people. Before long, the colonists spread to the mainland, where adventurers like Hernan Cortes destroyed the Aztec and Incan Empires. They inflicted widespread genocide on indigenous populations through violence and the introduction of new diseases. With the main threats to their rule crushed, the Spanish were free to ship vast sums of gold back to Europe along with new foodstuffs such as potatoes, tomatoes, and chocolate.

At the same time as this was happening, Spain expanded its interest in the Mediterranean, taking land in North Africa and Italy. Before long, it became a major global power.

Spain would rule millions of people in its colonies in America and beyond. However, its rivals soon took note of its success, and the Spanish spent enormous amounts of money fighting wars to defend their empire from other Europeans.

Ultimately, Spain overextended itself and went into economic decline. By the early seventeenth century, it struggled to match the newer empires of the English and the Dutch. By the nineteenth century, its American colonies had declared independence and fractured into many different states. However, the Spanish Empire controlled some of its territories for over 300 years, and we can still see the cultural effects of this today.[6]

What was the Levant Company?

The Levant Company was formed in 1592 by a merger of the Venice and Turkey Companies. It held a monopoly over English trade with the Ottoman Empire (based in modern Turkey). This meant that only members of the company were allowed to import goods from there into England. They mainly imported spices and other goods from Asia, making significant sums of money and earning a great deal of prestige.

The skills and resources that the company's members gathered were essential for later English expansion. For example, the Levant Company provided much of the initial leadership and some initial funds for the more famous East India Company.[7]

Section 2: Did Pirates start the British Empire?

Two popular works on the British Empire by Niall Ferguson and Jeremy Paxman, both entitled *Empire*, argue that the story of the empire begins with piracy and privateering.[8] Ferguson believes that when English expeditions to the Americas failed to find gold like the Spanish and Portuguese, they decided to rob the Spaniards instead.[9] This theory states that piracy remained vital until the seventeenth century, when the sugar trade surpassed it as the prime factor in British Imperialism.[10]

There is some merit in such an idea. However, we saw in the previous chapter that the British Empire was very complicated, making the idea of such a simple 'beginning' for it sound suspicious. Therefore, let us look at piracy as one of the multiple connected factors that helped start the British Empire.

Piracy and funds for investment

One way in which piracy certainly did help to develop the British Empire was by providing funds to be reinvested elsewhere. Privateering allowed many to make a profit, which they then used to support the development of the empire.[11] For example, the government turned plundering into a business, taking shares of the profits and selling the looted goods.[12] Beyond the share taken by the government, people who made their fortunes in piracy often reinvested their money in trading voyages to the East, further developing the British economy.[13] For example, Queen Elizabeth I invested cash that she had made backing Francis Drake's piracy in the newly formed Levant Company.[14]

Sometimes, privateers reinvested their funds in the Caribbean, where many of them practised their piracy. For instance, Henry Morgan invested his earnings in Jamaica.[15] Such spending had a significant impact on day-to-day life in Jamaica and helped give a big boost to agriculture on the island.[16] This is crucial, as Jamaica would play a big role in the British Empire of the eighteenth century.

Capturing bases: A reason and an opportunity

Hilary Beckles argues that the English first gained a foothold in the Caribbean by capturing Spanish bases.[17] These captures weren't always achieved directly through acts of piracy; the English captured Jamaica during a formal war with Spain in the 1650s.[18] However, Darwin and Mark Hanna have argued that one of the motivations for capturing such bases was to have somewhere to coordinate the raids against the Spanish.[19] Beyond this, piracy and conflict with the Spanish provided both the inspiration that led the English to consider settling in the Americas and skills that would help them in the long term.[20]

The lasting impact of piracy

The impact of piracy was not just limited to the age of famous Elizabethan privateers such as Francis Drake, Walter Raleigh, and John Hawkins. Pirates helped to build, finance, and defend the British Empire, and it was not until the 1690s that there was an official crackdown against them.[21] Even in the late seventeenth century, pirates had close ties to the colonial elite and were influential in developing colonial maritime communities.[22] For example, they helped to defend Jamaica from 1660, when for a time, the official navy was unable to do so.[23] English pirates, combined with the French and Dutch, did significant long-term damage to the Spanish Empire, thus weakening a major rival in the long term.[24]

Furthermore, pirates significantly impacted the maritime world's future, playing a major role in remapping the oceans into one continuous system. Previously, sailors viewed different oceans as separate bodies.[25] Pirates were also closely linked to the settlers and merchants of their time.[26] This last point is crucial, as it shows that although pirates were important, they were not the whole story.

Piracy was important, but it was not the only important thing going on

It seems clear that pirates did have quite a significant impact on the early British Empire. They played their part in gathering information, raising funds, weakening rivals, and capturing bases. However, there was no single path to building an empire.[27] Pirates were not the only people involved in the early stage of making the empire. They were not acting in isolation.

Other motivations

Pirates and privateers were not the first English people to search for wealth across the Atlantic. That honour goes to John Cabot's voyage to Newfoundland in the fifteenth century and the following voyages of fishermen seeking cod.[28]

Also, although the purpose of taking Spanish land in the Caribbean may well have been to have bases to raid and pillage from, there is an alternative interpretation. Anthony Pagden argues that Cromwell attempted to take the Spanish island Hispaniola (modern Cuba) as a base from which to capture, not pillage, other Spanish islands. Allegedly, part of his motivation for this was to spread his specific form of religion.[29] By this logic, Hispaniola was a steppingstone in Cromwell's holy war.

Perhaps even more significantly, privateers such as Drake and Hawkins initially attempted to be traders (specifically, slave traders) before their failures led them to turn to privateering.[30] It seems pretty clear that a lot was going on in the Americas that had little or nothing to do with piracy.

The adverse effects of piracy

In some ways, piracy may even have hindered the development of the empire. Although, as we have seen, pirates retained support from some nobles until the late seventeenth century, they were an embarrassment to the central government as early as the coronation of James I in 1601.[31]

Additionally, trade, rather than piracy, would have provided the best access to the Spanish Empire.[32] Piracy undermined this possibility during times of peace, leading to a breakdown in relations between England and Spain.[33] This led to a prolonged conflict between the two states that hurt early English attempts to settle in the Americas.[34] The obsession with plundering Spain that followed may even have slowed down these attempts even further.[35]

Judgement on piracy

While piracy did have a significant impact during the early stages of the empire, to argue that it was 'the' starting point of the empire would be misleading. Piracy was always one factor among many. It helped to forge the empire in some ways and hindered it in others. Some in power supported it, and others did not. It provided one route to gain wealth, but there were others, such as trade. In the next chapter, we'll take a more detailed look at how peaceful trade also played an essential part in the development of the British Empire.

---

[1] Sources:
Ferguson, N., *Empire: How Britain made the modern world*, Penguin edition (London: Penguin, 2004).
Lane, K. E., *Pillaging the empire: Global piracy on the high seas, 1500-1750*, 2nd edition (New York: Routledge, 2016).
McDonald, K. P., *Pirates, merchants, settlers, and slaves* (Oakland: University of California Press, 2015).
Paxman, J., *Empire*, Penguin edition (London: Penguin, 2012).
Rodger, N. A. M., *The Safeguard of the sea: A naval history of Britain 660-1649*, Kindle edition (London: Penguin, 2004).
Ronald, S., *The pirate queen: Queen Elizabeth I, her pirate adventurers and the dawn of empire* (London: HarperCollins, 2007).
Schama, S., *A history of Britain: At the edge of the world? 3000BC-AD1603*, Kindle edition (London: Bodley Head, 2009).

[2] Sources:

Bennett, M., *Cromwell at war: The Lord General and his military revolution* (London: I.B. Tauris, 2017).
Coward, B., *Oliver Cromwell*, Routledge edition (New York: Routledge, 2014).
Gaunt, P. *The English Civil War: A military history* (New York: I.B. Tauris, 2014).
Purkiss, D. *The English Civil War: A people's history*, Harper Perennial edition (London: Harper Perennial, 2010).
Roberts, C., Roberts, F. D., and Bisson, D., *A history of England: Volume 1*, 2 vols., 2nd edition (New York: Routledge, 2016).
Schama, S., *A history of Britain: The British Wars 1603-1776*, Kindle edition (London: Bodley Head, 2009).

[3] Sources:
Guy, J., *The Tudors: A very short introduction*, 2nd edition (New York: Oxford University Press, 2013).
Lee, S. J., *The reign of Elizabeth I, 1558-1603*, (Abingdon: Routledge, 2007).
Richards, J. M., *Elizabeth I*, (Abingdon: Routledge, 2012).
Ronald, S., *The pirate queen: Queen Elizabeth I, her pirate adventurers and the dawn of empire* (London: HarperCollins, 2007).
Schama, S., *A history of Britain: At the edge of the world? 3000BC-AD1603*, Kindle edition (London: Bodley Head, 2009).
Tombs, R., *The English and their history* (London: Allen Lane, 2014).

[4] Sources:
Lane, K. E., *Pillaging the empire: Global piracy on the high seas, 1500-1750*, 2nd edition (New York: Routledge, 2016).
Paxman, J., *Empire*, Penguin edition (London: Penguin, 2012).
Rodger, N. A. M., *The Safeguard of the sea: A naval history of Britain 660-1649*, Kindle edition (London: Penguin, 2004).
Ronald, S., *The pirate queen: Queen Elizabeth I, her pirate adventurers and the dawn of empire* (London: HarperCollins, 2007).
Schama, S., *A history of Britain: At the edge of the world? 3000BC-AD1603*, Kindle edition (London: Bodley Head, 2009).
Sullivan, A., *Britain's war against the slave trade: the operations of the Royal Navy's West African Squadron, 1807-1867* (Philadelphia: Frontline Books, 2020).
Wathen, B., *Sir Francis Drake: The construction of a hero* (Cambridge: D.S. Brewer, 2009).

[5] Sources:
Appleby, J. C., 'War, politics and colonization, 1558-1625', in *The Oxford History of the British Empire: Volume 1, the origins of the empire, British overseas enterprise to the close of the seventeenth century*, ed. by N. Canny, 5 vols (Oxford: Oxford University Press, 1998), pp. 55-78.

James, L., *The rise and fall of the British Empire*, new edition (London: Abacus, 1998).
Lane, K. E., *Pillaging the empire: Global piracy on the high seas, 1500-1750*, 2nd edition (New York: Routledge, 2016).
McDonald, K. P., *Pirates, merchants, settlers, and slaves* (Oakland: University of California Press, 2015).
Rodger, N. A. M., *The Safeguard of the sea: A naval history of Britain 660-1649*, Kindle edition (London: Penguin, 2004).
Ronald, S., *The pirate queen: Queen Elizabeth I, her pirate adventurers and the dawn of empire* (London: HarperCollins, 2007).
Sullivan, A. *Britain's war against the slave trade: the operations of the Royal Navy's West African Squadron, 1807-1867* (Philadelphia: Frontline Books, 2020).

[6] Sources:
Chapman, C., *A history of Spain* (Jovian Press, 2017).
Darwin, J., *After Tamerlane: The rise and fall of global empires, 1400-2000*, Penguin edition (London: Penguin, 2008).
Devereux, A. W., *The other side of empire: Just war in the Mediterranean and the rise of early modern Spain* (Cornell University Press, 2020).
Frankopan, P., *The silk roads: A new history of the world*, paperback edition (London: Bloomsbury, 2016).
Maltby, W., *The rise and fall of the Spanish Empire* (Basingstoke: Palgrave Macmillan, 2009).
Wood, M., *Conquistadors*, new paperback edition (London: BBC Books, 2010).

[7] Sources:
Appleby, J. C., 'War, politics and colonization, 1558-1625', in *The Oxford History of the British Empire: Volume 1, the origins of the empire, British overseas enterprise to the close of the seventeenth century*, ed. by N. Canny, 5 vols (Oxford: Oxford University Press, 1998), pp. 55-78.
Dalziel, N., *The Penguin historical atlas of the British Empire* (London: Penguin, 2006).
Darwin, J., *Unfinished empire: The global expansion of Britain*, Penguin edition (London: Penguin, 2013).
James, L., *The rise and fall of the British Empire*, new edition (London: Abacus, 1998).
Laidlaw, C. *The British in the Levant: trade and perceptions of the Ottoman Empire in the eighteenth century* (New York: I. B. Tauris, 2010).
Marshall, P. J., 'The English in Asia to 1700', in *The Oxford History of the British Empire: Volume 1, the origins of the empire, British overseas enterprise to the close of the seventeenth century*, ed. by N. Canny, 5 vols (Oxford: Oxford University Press, 1998), pp. 264-285.

[8] N. Ferguson, *Empire: How Britain made the modern world*, Penguin edition (London: Penguin, 2004), pp. 1-14; J. Paxman, *Empire*, Penguin edition (London: Penguin, 2012), pp. 16-21.
[9] Ferguson, *Empire*, pp. 1-7.
[10] Ferguson, *Empire*, pp. 12-14; Paxman, *Empire*, pp. 20-21.
[11] A. Finucane, *The temptations of trade: Britain, Spain and the struggle for empire* (Philadelphia: University of Philadelphia Press, 2016), p. 1; L. James, *The rise and fall of the British Empire*, new edition (London: Abacus, 1998), p. 5.
[12] S. Ronald, *The pirate queen: Queen Elizabeth I, her pirate adventurers and the dawn of empire* (London: HarperCollins, 2007), chapter 39.
[13] Ronald, *The pirate queen*, chapter 39.
[14] N. A. M. Rodger, *The Safeguard of the sea: A naval history of Britain 660-1649*, Kindle edition (London: Penguin, 2004), p. 244.
[15] Ferguson, *Empire*, pp. 11-12.
[16] H. McD. Beckles, 'The "Hub of Empire": The Caribbean and Britain in the seventeenth century', in *The Oxford History of the British Empire: Volume 1, the origins of the empire, British overseas enterprise to the close of the seventeenth century*, ed. by N. Canny, 5 vols (Oxford: Oxford University Press, 1998), (pp. 218-240); M. J. Braddick, 'The English government, war, trade and settlement, 1625-1688', in *The Oxford History of the British Empire: Volume 1, the origins of the empire, British overseas enterprise to the close of the seventeenth century*, ed. by N. Canny, 5 vols (Oxford: Oxford University Press, 1998), pp. 287-308, (p.296).
[17] Beckles, 'Hub of Empire', p. 218.
[18] Braddick, 'The English government', p. 286.
[19] J. Darwin, *Unfinished empire: The global expansion of Britain*, Penguin edition (London: Penguin, 2013), p. 36; M. G. Hanna, *Pirate nests and the rise of the British Empire, 1570-1740* (Chapel Hill: The University of North Carolina press, 2015), p. 102.
[20] J. C. Appleby, 'War, politics and colonization, 1558-1625', in *The Oxford History of the British Empire: Volume 1, the origins of the empire, British overseas enterprise to the close of the seventeenth century*, ed. by N. Canny, 5 vols (Oxford: Oxford University Press, 1998), pp. 55-78, (pp. 61-62, 70).
[21] M. Rediker, 'Pirates and the imperial state', review of *Captain Kidd and the war against pirates*, by R. C. Ritchie, *Reviews in American History*, 16.3 (1988), 351-357, (pp. 354-55).
[22] Hanna, *Pirate nests*, pp. 1-4.
[23] Hanna, *Pirate nests*, p. 102.
[24] K. E. Lane, *Pillaging the empire: Global piracy on the high seas, 1500-1750*, 2nd edition (New York: Routledge, 2016), introduction.
[25] K. P. McDonald, *Pirates, merchants, settlers, and slaves* (Oakland: University of California Press, 2015), p. 3.
[26] McDonald, *Pirates, merchants, settlers*, p. 4.
[27] Finucane, *The temptations of trade*, p. 9.

[28] E. L. Cox, review of *Trade, plunder and settlement: Maritime enterprise and the Genesis of the British Empire, 1480-1630*, by K. R. Andrews, *The International History Review*, 8.4 (1986), 625-627; N. Dalziel, *The Penguin historical atlas of the British Empire* (London: penguin, 2006), p. 14.

[29] A. Pagden, 'The struggle for legitimacy and the image of empire in the Atlantic to c.1700', in *The Oxford History of the British Empire: Volume 1, the origins of the empire, British overseas enterprise to the close of the seventeenth century*, ed. by N. Canny, 5 vols (Oxford: Oxford University Press, 1998), pp. 34-54, (p. 35).

[30] James, *Rise and fall*, p. 16; Lane, *Pillaging the empire*, chapter 2.

[31] Rodger, *Safeguard of the sea*, pp. 347-48.

[32] Finucane, *The temptations of trade*, p. 9.

[33] Finucane, *The temptations of trade*, p. 19; Rodger, *Safeguard of the sea*, p. 200.

[34] James, *Rise and fall*, p. 5.

[35] Cox, review of Andrews, p. 627.

Chapter 5: Trade

Section 1: Introduction and Explanations

Piracy obviously had its part to play, but there are limits to how far pirates (even government-backed privateers) could go in creating an empire. Another crucial starting point for the British Empire was international trade. In the fifteenth and sixteenth centuries, the world of trade opened up, and there were opportunities for European merchants that didn't involve robbing their Spanish neighbours.

If we're discussing the wider world, then it's only right that I have a few explanations concerning some of the other important world empires in this period. First up is Portugal. Like the Spanish, they also beat the English to starting an empire. Unlike the Spanish, their empire was heavily based on trade in Africa and Asia rather than the Americas. The Portuguese played a key role in discovering new trade routes, and it is impossible to fully understand the early British Empire without knowing a little about these pioneers.

Of course, European traders needed someone to trade with. For that reason, I've written an explanation of the Ottoman Empire, while the one on the Mughal Empire from the first chapter is also highly relevant.

Finally, it is hard to think about trade and the British Empire without considering the East India Company, so make sure that you check that one out.

What was the Portuguese Empire?

The Portuguese Empire was the first of the global European empires. Surrounded by Spain on land and excluded from the lucrative Mediterranean trade by powerful Italian states such as Venice and Genoa, the Portuguese turned to the Atlantic.

They began by colonising small islands nestled in the ocean, then pushed south along the African coastline. They created strong trade links, built, or captured, forts to protect their investments and became involved in the gold trade, the caravan trade, and pearl fishing.

There were darker elements to the Portuguese Empire, of course. The slave trade was essential to the early growth of Portuguese imperialism, and when the King of Kongo begged them to stop their slaving, they refused out of hand. Similarly, they sometimes behaved with utterly senseless brutality, once burning a ship full of Muslim pilgrims.

In 1498 Vasco da Gama sailed around the African coast and landed in India, discovering for Portugal an extremely lucrative trade route that could provide spices and all manner of valuables from the East. Portugal's Indian exploits would inspire later empires like the British and the Dutch. However, Portugal didn't have everything easy; many ships that tried to copy da Gama never returned home. Similarly, European rivals considered the Portuguese prime targets, and many privateers preyed on their shipping.

As the Spanish copied the success of their neighbours, the Pope got involved. He drew a line, dividing the world between the two powers. This gave Spain control of the Americas and protected Portugal's interests in Africa and Asia. However, Portugal would later discover that this division also granted them rule of Brazil, which Europeans had not found at the time of the treaty.

By the sixteenth century, Portugal controlled a commercial empire extending from Brazil to the China Sea. But their time at the pinnacle of European power was brief.

Over time, the French, Dutch, and British caught up with and overtook the Portuguese. As early as the seventeenth century, other Europeans saw the Portuguese Empire as backwards and outdated. In some places, like Brazil, the Portuguese remained strong throughout the eighteenth century, but rivals picked their empire apart in other areas, including much of Asia. In the nineteenth century, the British and Germans invested heavily in Portugal's remaining colonies and essentially took control of them. Despite this, the Portuguese did not surrender the last remnants of their colonial empire, such as Macau, until late in the twentieth century.[1]

What was the Ottoman Empire?

The Ottoman Empire was based in what is now Turkey. Although it was primarily an Islamic country, its rulers (Sultans) granted some autonomy to religious minorities to try to win their acceptance.

The Ottomans had a humble beginning. In the year 1300, they were nothing more than a minor chiefdom. However, they expanded considerably over the coming centuries. In 1453 they captured Byzantium, one of the great Christian cities. Following this, they spread into Europe, Egypt, and Ethiopia in the West and expanded their interests in the East.

Military victories brought commercial dominance in the Mediterranean, which the Ottomans combined with heavy taxation to become an economic powerhouse. This wealth allowed them to launch many construction programmes, and they built mosques, hospitals, roads, aqueducts, and much more.

Over time, as international trade became dominated by European ships instead of the ancient land-based routes, the Ottoman Empire began to struggle. By the late seventeenth century, the empire was shrinking and faced many internal and external threats.

Although there were multiple attempts at reform and the empire survived in some form until the early twentieth century, it was a shell of its former self in its later years. Its power in international politics had diminished considerably, and its citizens had quite a poor quality of life, with life expectancy very low.[2]

What was the East India Company?

The East India Company was an English trading company chartered by Queen Elizabeth I. It held a monopoly on the trade between England and the East Indies, importing goods to be re-exported to mainland Europe at a profit.

In its early years, it focused on setting up factories to trade relatively peacefully. It had a rivalry with the Dutch East India Company, but it overcame this through a deal that allowed it to focus on textiles while the Dutch concentrated on spices. However, the company changed significantly over time.

Increasingly, it became more aggressive and started to get involved in successful military operations against Indian rulers. They first secured tax collection rights before eventually becoming political leaders. They also diversified the goods they traded, importing increasing quantities of tea from China and selling opium back to the Chinese people (despite the best efforts of the Qing government in China to stop this).

In 1833, following repeated scandals, the company lost its trade monopoly. It was later dissolved entirely as the British government took direct control of India.[3]

Section 2: The role of foreign trade

In the last chapter, we saw that piracy was important to the development of the British Empire but was only one part of the puzzle. In this chapter, we will look at another piece of the puzzle, international trade. I aim to show that trade was important before piracy, remained significant throughout the golden age of piracy in the sixteenth and seventeenth centuries, and had great long-term significance for the empire.

Humble beginnings

Before the late sixteenth century, English international trade was meagre, and few Englishmen had overseas interests.[4] This changed when Elizabeth I saw the distinct advantages that Spain had gained through such commerce.[5] However, this also posed a problem. England was a latecomer in European exploration and trade, so it would have to challenge the dominance developed by Spain, Portugal, and the Dutch.[6]

Atlantic trade and links to piracy

Despite these limitations, international trade did exist in England before the golden age of privateering and would continue throughout it. As we have already discovered, famous pirates Francis Drake and John Hawkins began as slave traders before circumstances forced them into piracy.[7] In fact, in the years before the war with Spain (of Spanish Armada fame), English overseas actions focused on exploring, trading, and attempting to set up plantations.[8] England tried to break into the gold, ivory, and pepper trade of West Africa, and their ultimate goal was to access trade with the Spanish Empire.[9]

There is strong evidence that these attempts at trading led to conflict and piracy. Britain's entry into existing markets led to tension, which in turn, led to conflict.[10] For example, Hawkins' attempts at slaving increased tensions between England and Spain, leading to a rise in piracy and privateering.[11]

Part of this may have been a conscious decision. Historians such as Nicholas Rodger and Nigel Dalziel have argued that privateering was partly motivated by a desire to break into Spain's monopoly.[12] Military action was one way for England to overcome its weaknesses and get the trade it wanted.[13] In short, trade, piracy, and later, settlement were all interdependent; England needed all of them to build its empire.[14]

Trade across the globe

So far, we have mostly looked at the Atlantic and England's rivalry with Spain in the Americas. But England's trade extended far beyond the Atlantic Ocean. When the Pope excommunicated Elizabeth I, this opened up commerce with the Islamic Ottoman Empire in the Mediterranean; it was here that they would learn valuable skills such as how to trade with a mighty empire.[15] The English continued to trade peacefully in the Levant region of the Eastern Mediterranean even while piracy was rising in the Atlantic.

Likewise, the experience and wealth gained by the Levant Company continued to help English and British traders over the coming centuries. The company even paid the expenses of diplomacy with the Ottomans until 1804 and provided some leadership and initial funding for the East India Company.[16]

Trade went much further afield than the Mediterranean, however. The English were still exploring and looking for new trade routes to China.[17] Europeans demanded various goods from Asia, such as silk, cotton textiles, and porcelain.[18] The elites craved such luxuries, and merchants saw them as a way of getting rich.[19] The East India Company was formed in 1600 to bring back valuables like these and advance the cause of English trade more broadly.[20]

We must be cautious not to overstate the significance of this, of course. At this point, the company was a far cry from what it would later become. Its initial charter banned it from conquest and colonisation, and the real expansion of European trade in Asia did not come until after 1630.[21] However, the Company's foundation is an early sign of expanding British interest in Asia. A particular area of specialism for England was the trade of Indian cloth.[22] Indian textiles were especially useful for the English as they became valuable commodities in the slave trade, being bartered for captives on the West African Coast.[23]

Things were not always peaceful. The Dutch and Portuguese were already well established in the East before the English arrived.[24] England came into conflict with the Dutch over trading rights for spices in South-East Asia and the Portuguese over India.[25] They also attempted to fight the Mughal Empire but soon realised their mistake and made peace. They would not fight an open war in India again for a long time; it was simply too expensive.[26]

There were also ties between trade in the East and Atlantic piracy. Tales of adventure such as Francis Drake's circumnavigation of the globe helped create widespread excitement for an expansion to the East.[27] But, trading was expensive and risky. Only large groups of merchants or governments could afford it.[28]

The relative prices of precious metals in Asia and Europe meant that Europeans tended to buy Asian goods in bullion rather than bartering for them.[29] Therefore, merchants could use bullion captured in the Atlantic to purchase Eastern goods, which worked out incredibly well considering investors wanted to diversify rather than just focus on the Atlantic.[30]

English law at the time banned the export of silver bullion, and critics believed this trade harmed the economy.[31] However, the East India Company's charter granted it a special compensation to export bullion, demonstrating the growing importance of commerce in Asia and the necessity of bullion to make it a success.[32] Therefore, English trading interests were undoubtedly not eclipsed by piracy. The two went hand in hand.

The lasting impact of trade

International trade was essential for the British Empire in the long term. We have already discussed some potential motivations for Cromwell's attempts to capture Spanish lands in the West Indies, exploring whether he was capturing islands to spread religion or capturing them to use as raiding bases. However, when we look at Cromwell's later actions, we can see that trade was clearly important in his mind.

He passed Navigation Acts, which ensured British ships would control commerce with the West Indies.[33] This became a crucial imperial policy. By the late seventeenth century, Britain was increasingly determined to monopolise trade with the colonies, ensuring they were the ones to reap the rewards from their territories.[34] Trade with the West Indies and mainland American colonies earned Britain a vast amount of money, though, over time, trade with Asia would rival it.[35] In short, the future of the British Empire was very much about controlling and expanding commerce.

---

[1] Sources:
Darwin, J., *After Tamerlane: The rise and fall of global empires, 1400-2000*, Penguin edition (London: Penguin, 2008).
Frankopan, P., *The silk roads: A new history of the world*, paperback edition (London: Bloomsbury, 2016).
Newitt, M., *Portugal in European and world history* (London: Reaktion Books, 2009).
Roberts, J. M., and Westad, O. A., *The Penguin history of the world*, 6th edition (London: Penguin, 2013).
Subrahmanyam, S., *The Portuguese Empire in Asia, 1500-1700*, 2nd edition (Chichester: Wiley, 2012).

[2] Sources:
Ágoston, G., *The last Muslim conquest: The Ottoman Empire and its wars in Europe* (Woodstock: Princeton University Press, 2021).

Darwin, J., *After Tamerlane: The rise and fall of global empires, 1400-2000*, Penguin edition (London: Penguin, 2008).
Frankopan, P., *The silk roads: A new history of the world*, paperback edition (London: Bloomsbury, 2016).
Şükrü Hanioğlu, M., *A brief history of the late Ottoman Empire* (Woodstock: Princeton University Press, 2008).
Yildiz, A., *Crisis and rebellion in the Ottoman Empire: The downfall of a Sultan in the Age of Revolution* (London: I.B. Tauris, 2017).
Quataert, D., *The Ottoman Empire, 1700-1922*, 2nd edition (New York: Cambridge University Press, 2005).

[3] Sources:
Darwin, J., *Unfinished empire: The global expansion of Britain*, Penguin edition (London: Penguin, 2013).
Ferguson, N., *Empire: How Britain made the modern world*, Penguin edition (London: Penguin, 2004).
Hunt, T. *Ten cities that made an empire*, Penguin edition (London: Penguin, 2015).
Lawson, P. *The East India Company: A history*, new edition (New York: Routledge, 2013).
Pettigrew, W. A., and Gopalan, M., 'Introduction: The different East India Companies and the variety of cross-cultural interactions in the corporate setting', in *The East India Company, 1600-1857: Essays on Anglo-Indian connection*, ed. by W. A. Pettigrew and M. Gopalan, (New York: Routledge, 2017).
Schama, S., *A history of Britain: The British Wars 1603-1776*, Kindle edition (London: Bodley Head, 2009).

[4] J. C. Appleby, 'War, politics and colonization, 1558-1625', in *The Oxford History of the British Empire: Volume 1, the origins of the empire, British overseas enterprise to the close of the seventeenth century*, ed. by N. Canny, 5 vols (Oxford: Oxford University Press, 1998), pp. 55-78, (p. 55); Canny, N. 'The origins of empire: An introduction', in *The Oxford History of the British Empire: Volume 1, the origins of the empire, British overseas enterprise to the close of the seventeenth century*, ed. by N. Canny, 5 vols (Oxford: Oxford University Press, 1998), pp. 1-33, (p. 3).
[5] Canny, 'Origins of empire', p. 4.
[6] Appleby, 'War, politics, colonization', pp. 56, 76.
[7] L. James, *The rise and fall of the British Empire*, new edition (London: Abacus, 1998), p. 16; K. E. Lane, *Pillaging the empire: Global piracy on the high seas, 1500-1750*, 2nd edition (New York: Routledge, 2016), chapter 2.
[8] Appleby, 'War, politics, colonization', p. 59.

[9] Appleby, 'War, politics, colonization', p. 59; A. Finucane, *The temptations of trade: Britain, Spain and the struggle for empire* (Philadelphia: University of Philadelphia Press, 2016), p. 2.

[10] M. J. Braddick, 'The English government, war, trade and settlement, 1625-1688', in *The Oxford History of the British Empire: Volume 1, the origins of the empire, British overseas enterprise to the close of the seventeenth century*, ed. by N. Canny, 5 vols (Oxford: Oxford University Press, 1998), pp. 287-308, (pp. 292-93), on tension.

[11] Appleby, 'War, politics, colonization', pp. 59-60.

[12] N. Dalziel, *The Penguin historical atlas of the British Empire* (London: Penguin, 2006), p. 23; N. A. M. Rodger, *The Safeguard of the sea: A naval history of Britain 660-1649*, Kindle edition (London: Penguin, 2004), chapter 15.

[13] A. Games, *The web of empire: English cosmopolitans in an age of expansion, 1560-1660* (New York: Oxford University Press, 2008), p. 8.

[14] E. L. Cox, review of *Trade, plunder and settlement: Maritime enterprise and the Genesis of the British Empire, 1480-1630*, by K. R. Andrews, *The International History Review*, 8.4 (1986), 625-627, (p.627).

[15] Games, *Web of empire*, pp. 50-51.

[16] Appleby, 'War, politics, colonization', pp. 60-61; Dalziel, *Penguin historical atlas*, pp. 22-23; C. Laidlaw, *The British in the Levant: trade and perceptions of the Ottoman Empire in the eighteenth century* (New York: I. B. Tauris, 2010), p. 1; James, *Rise and fall*, p. 25; P. J., Marshall, 'The English in Asia to 1700', in *The Oxford History of the British Empire: Volume 1, the origins of the empire, British overseas enterprise to the close of the seventeenth century*, ed. by N. Canny, 5 vols (Oxford: Oxford University Press, 1998), pp. 264-285, (p. 267).

[17] Appleby, 'War, politics, colonization', p. 62.

[18] Marshall, 'English in Asia', p. 264.

[19] Lawson, P. *The East India Company: A history*, new edition (New York: Routledge, 2013), chapter 1.

[20] T. Hunt, *Ten cities that made an empire*, Penguin edition (London: Penguin, 2015), p. 190.

[21] K. N. Chaudhuri, *The trading world of Asia and the English East India Company, 1660-1760*, paperback edition (Cambridge: Cambridge University Press, 2006) p. 7; Lawson, *East India Company*, Chapter 2; Pettigrew, W. A. and Gopalan, M., 'Introduction: The different East India Companies and the variety of cross-cultural interactions in the corporate setting', in *The East India Company, 1600-1857: Essays on Anglo-Indian connection*, ed. by W. A. Pettigrew and M. Gopalan, (New York: Routledge, 2017).

[22] Marshall, 'English in Asia', p. 275.

[23] James, *Rise and fall*, pp. 24-25.

[24] Hunt, *Ten cities*, p. 190; James, *Rise and fall*, pp. 25-6.

[25] Marshall, 'English in Asia', pp. 270-73.

[26] Hunt, *Ten cities*, p. 189; Marshall, 'English in Asia', pp. 280-81.

[27] Lawson, *East India Company*, chapter 1.
[28] Marshall, 'English in Asia', p. 266.
[29] Lawson, *East India Company*, chapter 1; Marshall, 'English in Asia', p. 269.
[30] Games, *Web of empire*, p.83; Marshall, 'English in Asia', p. 264.
[31] Chaudhuri, *Trading world*, p. 8; Lawson, *East India Company*, chapter 1.
[32] Lawson, *East India Company*, chapter 2.
[33] H., McD. Beckles, "The 'Hub of Empire": The Caribbean and Britain in the seventeenth century', in *The Oxford History of the British Empire: Volume 1, the origins of the empire, British overseas enterprise to the close of the seventeenth century*, ed. by N. Canny, 5 vols (Oxford: Oxford University Press, 1998), pp. 218-240, (p. 236).
[34] Canny, 'Origins of empire', pp. 22-23.
[35] Marshall, 'English in Asia', pp. 283-84.

Chapter 6: Colonies in the Americas

Section 1: Introduction and Explanations

So far, we've mostly been looking at informal forms of imperialism. Now, it's time to move on to more formal means of control. The primary purpose of this chapter is to discuss why England tried to colonise the Americas. However, this is quite a big topic. While I can guide you through it, you'll need a lot of background knowledge to appreciate its subtleties and, most importantly, form your own conclusions. For that reason, there are six explanations in this chapter.

First, we'll look at two key early colonies, Jamestown and Roanoke. Then, we'll discuss two of the men behind these colonies, John Smith and Sir Walter Raleigh. The next explanation will give some brief information on the Virginia Company. Finally, there's a short section explaining what Puritanism is. If you have some knowledge of all these, it will make it much easier for you to form your opinion on why England wanted colonies in the Americas.

What was Jamestown?

Jamestown was the first successful English colony in North America. It was founded in Virginia in 1607 and funded by a group of merchants and aristocrats. Many hoped the settlement would bring riches to England by trading with the region's indigenous people and searching for gold. Despite some fears over the venture caused by earlier failures, parliament was very enthusiastic about it, and King James I gave his backing.

The expedition was led by John Smith, an experienced soldier and adventurer. Smith proved to be a competent leader, and initially, things looked to be going well. The project had been planned thoroughly, and the colonists took many tools and medical supplies with them. Likewise, initial contact with the Native Americans was friendly as the English settlers began to trade the vast amount of copper they had brought for food. The local people vastly outnumbered the English, so they probably did not initially view the newcomers as threats. However, things soon took a turn for the worse.

Cultural differences between the English and the Native Americans began to cause problems. The English punished any petty thefts extremely harshly, something which horrified the Native Americans. Likewise, the English traded far too much of their copper too quickly, which devalued it. Their willingness to deal directly with the Native American people rather than allowing the local chief Powhatan to control trade also angered him.

Hunger set in. The colonists found it much harder to hunt game or catch fish than they had expected. Five months after the expedition had arrived, only 46 of the initial 104 colonists still lived. The situation was so dire that they had to resort to cannibalism. Hunger and starvation remained a threat to the colony for several years. Jamestown's leaders, therefore, enforced a harsh discipline system to ensure the colony's survival, with death being the punishment for many crimes.

Eventually, tobacco planting saved the colony (and colonisation in Virginia more generally). Mass production of this plant made the colony profitable and secured its future. This did have some negative consequences, however. It made the territory much more expansionist, leading to more conflicts with the Native Americans as the settlers drove them from their land.[1]

What was Roanoke?

The colony at Roanoke Island was one of the earliest English attempts to colonise the Americas. Sir Walter Raleigh planned the expedition and chose the location for the settlement. He selected it because he considered it far enough away from Spanish bases to prevent it from being destroyed by Spanish raiders but close enough to allow the English to attack Spanish shipping. Raleigh also hoped to find precious metals there. However, the colony faced many difficulties.

Although initial contact with the indigenous people of Roanoke had been friendly, they soon came to resent the English presence on their island. Likewise, the colony severely lacked funding and support from England. Although Queen Elizabeth I was initially very enthusiastic about the project, she later lost interest. With the English engaged in a war with Spain, communications between Roanoke and England were difficult, and supplies became very limited.

Francis Drake was able to take away some of the starving or injured colonists on the way back from one of his voyages in the Caribbean. Those who remained behind vanished without a trace. To this day, nobody knows for sure what happened to them.[2]

Who was Sir Walter Raleigh?

Sir Walter Raleigh was an Elizabethan courtier and pirate. He fought as a soldier in Ireland and became the Vice-Admiral of Devon, using his natural charm to rise through the social ranks. For example, he named Virginia in America after the unmarried Queen Elizabeth I. By winning the queen's favour, Raleigh gained significant wealth and power. Despite this, his thick West-Country accent was always a black mark against him in the social hierarchy of his age.

Raleigh was anti-Catholic and anti-Spanish. He wanted to harm Spanish interests and believed that the Americas could provide England with great wealth. This led him to become one of the main drivers of English expansion in the New World. Unfortunately, he did not have a great deal of personal success. As well as the failed colony at Roanoke, he organised unsuccessful attempts to find the fabled city of gold, El Dorado.

Although his career depended on royal favour, he did not always have it. In 1593 Queen Elizabeth had him thrown in the Tower of London when he secretly got married and lied to her about it. She ultimately forgave him, but this was not the end of Raleigh's problems with royal authority. When Elizabeth died and James I took the throne, Raleigh was found guilty of high treason and ultimately sentenced to death.

He was a man of contrasts, both made and broken by royal authority. Although his exploits had a significant impact on the British Empire, he died before he could see any of this really start to take shape.[3]

Who was John Smith?

John Smith was the first leader of the Jamestown colony in Virginia. He was a colourful character. He fought as a mercenary for the Austrians against the Ottoman Turks, getting captured and sold into slavery. Even after securing his freedom, his career was turbulent. While sailing across the Atlantic on the Jamestown voyage, Smith was accused of mutiny and imprisoned. However, when the expedition arrived in America, sealed orders from the Virginia Company were opened, revealing that the Company had chosen Smith to lead the colony.

Smith was a generally good leader. He won the respect of Powhatan, the leader of the local Native Americans, and enforced the discipline necessary for the struggling colony to survive. After he returned to England, the starvation faced by the colonists got much worse, suggesting that Smith's leadership had been crucial in Jamestown's early survival.

Smith firmly believed that the English needed to build an empire in the Americas to ensure their society had a promising future. As such, he became involved with several more attempts to colonise the Americas.[4]

What was the Virginia Company?

The Virginia Company was a London-based company made up of a variety of merchants and aristocrats. It was formed in 1606 and aimed to establish English colonies in the Americas. It founded the Jamestown colony, hoping to make a profit by finding gold and trading with the Native Americans. While the colonists failed to find gold and relationships with the Native Americans soon soured, the colony eventually became profitable by planting tobacco.

The Virginia Company aggressively promoted its colony by using sermons and lotteries. It also appealed to religious groups by stating they intended to convert Native Americans to Christianity.

However, the Company faced many internal issues. Its members were divided between those who wanted to pursue short-term profit and those who prioritised long-term gain. This was unsustainable, and in 1624 the Company collapsed. However, many of its former members continued to be involved in colonisation efforts.[5]

Who were Puritans?

Puritans were radical Protestant Christians. The word 'puritan' originated as a term of abuse given to zealous Christians who believed themselves to be 'the Godly' but whose radical views were disapproved of by rulers like Elizabeth I and Charles I. Eventually, puritans adopted the word as their own and became proud of it.

Puritans wanted to eradicate any traces of Catholicism from the English church. At times, they were willing to participate in the broader, official Anglican forms of worship while also undertaking their specific rituals at home. At other times, they were more actively resistant. They particularly disliked Charles I and Archbishop Laud's reforms of the Anglican church, including Charles' defence of holding traditional festivals on a Sunday, which they intensely disliked. This contributed to many puritans fighting for parliament against Charles during the English Civil War.

Although puritans were united against the religious practices of Charles I, they shared no agreement about exactly how Christianity should be practised, leading to many fractures.[6]

Section 2: Why did England want colonies in the Americas?

This is a difficult question because, as we have seen, English imperialism was made up of many individuals, each with their own interests.[7] There were differences between the state and individuals, as well as changes across time and place. Despite this, we can draw out some key motives that led both the English state and the English people to seek new land across the Atlantic. These include the chance to expand the state and diversify the economy, opportunities to make money, and the prospect of a better life. Therefore, the overarching motivation for seeking land in the Americas was simply that the Americas offered unlimited opportunities. Whatever people wanted, they believed that they could find it across the ocean.

There were some links to Spain, pirates, and trade

Firstly, there is evidence that some politicians aimed to copy Spain's success.[8] Likewise, some bases, such as the failed colony at Roanoke and arguably Jamestown in Virginia, were partly motivated by a desire to raid Spain.[9]

However, we must be careful not to overstate the links. Not everyone agrees that its relationship with Spain defined the location of England's early colonies. For instance, some historians don't agree that Jamestown's founders intended it to be a raiding base.[10] Likewise, the early bases in the Caribbean were also in very unsuitable locations to be used for pillaging.[11] In fact, focussing on privateering and plundering likely diverted resources away from attempting to create permanent settlements.[12]

Still, in the long run, the experience gained by English privateers probably helped the colonies to develop.[13] Therefore, although it is unclear how much credit we can give to piracy as a motivator to found colonies, it still quite obviously had an impact on the fledgling colonies once they gained a foothold.

Colonies were also linked to trade. Some historians believe that Jamestown's founders hoped it would become a trading hub, doing business with the Native Americans and providing a safe base for merchants on the way to China.[14] However, as with piracy, not all historians agree on this.[15]

One crucial fact that we need to remember is that the Jamestown colony only became successful after tobacco was planted and used as a cash crop. This suggests that it failed as a trading hub, though it also shows that the colony did help trade more broadly by providing goods to sell.[16] So, whatever its initial founders planned, Jamestown's long-term development was largely a result of it finding an important role in global trade.

The hunt for precious metals

Most, if not all, of the early English attempts at colonising the New World were at least partially motivated by the desire to find gold and silver as Spain had.[17] This was true of Roanoke, as well as the early settlements in the Caribbean and at Jamestown.[18] Many Jamestown settlers were so preoccupied with hunting for gold that they prioritised the search over providing for their survival.[19] Over time, the drive to find gold came to be replaced by investments in agriculture, but it was undoubtedly a significant initial motivation.[20]

The chance for a fresh start

The Virginia Company used sermons and lotteries to promote their venture in Jamestown, while the Caribbean was marketed as a place where people of all classes would find opportunities.[21] This was important in a society that believed all labourers had a moral obligation to work.[22] It was especially important given that the social make-up of England was changing during this period. The Enclosure Act allowed aristocrats to make exclusive use of formerly shared land. This forced extended families to shrink, and thus some peripheral members such as younger sons were forced to seek work elsewhere.[23]

Settler colonies in the Americas provided opportunities for those who were 'unwanted' or marginalised in Britain. Since people were used to travelling to find work, it is easy to see why many leapt at this opportunity.[24] This also benefited those in power, who saw it as a way of getting rid of potential troublemakers.[25]

Economic opportunities for England

The government had far more to gain from the Americas than a dumping ground for people they didn't want in England. It also provided an opportunity for them to diversify England's economy.[26] For example, the primary motivation for colonising Newfoundland was its abundant supply of cod.[27]

Walter Raleigh hoped that the American colonies would produce raw materials to export to England, where they would be turned into manufactured goods. This would, in turn, help to boost employment in England.[28] It would also mean that the English could now produce goods that had previously been imported from rival states.[29] There was even an overly optimistic hope that Virginia could make every type of trade good imaginable.[30]

The potential riches on offer were a powerful motive behind colonisation and were often used to promote the Virginia Company and its ventures.[31] Given that investors in England funded the Jamestown colony, there was clearly a hope that the American colonies would provide for those left in England as well as those actually in the colonies.[32]

State expansion

There were social and political as well as economic opportunities to be found in the Americas. Many at the time feared that the hot climate of the Caribbean would interfere with traditional English society.[33] That this concern existed shows that some in England wanted the colonies to be like an extension of England. Aristocrats, for example, saw the Caribbean as a new arena to compete for Royal patronage.[34]

This influenced the plans for the colonies' legal systems. The colony's backers wanted Jamestown's laws to be similar to those in England, with governing councils in both Virginia and England inextricably linking the two.[35] While initial Royal Charters allowed the early colonies a fair amount of autonomy, this didn't last long.[36] Over time, regulations such as the 1651 Navigation Act subordinated the colonies to the English Parliament and enforced increasingly tight controls.[37]

Religious ambitions and separatism

Although lots of travellers to the Americas went in search of wealth, there were also many religious and constitutional objectors.[38] The New World gave opportunities to those who were marginalised in Britain, and this included religious dissidents.[39]

An influential group of Puritan aristocrats worked together on multiple attempts to colonise the New World. Many corresponded with the early New England colony at Massachusetts Bay, founded by the Puritans of the famous 'Mayflower'.[40]

The Mayflower colonists wanted to create a 'Godly agrarian world' different to the Europe they had left behind.[41] When diseases spread among the Native Americans, they saw this as a sign, thinking that God was clearing the land for them.[42] It is unsurprising then that many New Englanders emphasised their separation from England. At times, they went so far as to act as if they were completely independent.[43]

But we must not overstate separatism

Although this was the attitude of some colonists, it was certainly not the attitude of all of them, even among the New England settlers. Firstly, the Mayflower carried many more moderate Protestants along with the Puritan 'Pilgrim Fathers'.[44] They weren't all religious zealots. Likewise, there was a hope among the Council for New England (a group of Puritan merchants) that the act of colonising new England would show those in England the error of their ways.[45] Although some believed the Church of England was too corrupt, many other settlers thought it could still be reformed.[46]

The New World was full of possibilities

There was a wide variety of motivations to colonise the Americas. Different groups had different interests, but even within groups such as religious dissidents, there was a range of opinions. Therefore, what was really important was the world of possibilities opened up by the Americas.

---

[1] Sources:
Chet, G., *The colonists' American Revolution: Preserving English liberty, 1607-1783* (Hoboken: Wiley Blackwell, 2020).
Darwin, J., *Unfinished empire: The global expansion of Britain*, Penguin edition (London: Penguin, 2013).
Ferguson, N., *Empire: How Britain made the modern world*, Penguin edition (London: Penguin, 2004).
James, L., *The rise and fall of the British Empire*, new edition (London: Abacus, 1998).
Kehoe, A. B., *North America before the European invasions*, 2nd edition (Abingdon: Routledge, 2017).
Perdue, T., and Green, M., *North American Indians: A very short introduction* (New York: Oxford University Press, 2010).

[2] Sources:

Dalziel, N., *The Penguin historical atlas of the British Empire* (London: Penguin, 2006).
Darwin, J., *Unfinished empire: The global expansion of Britain*, Penguin edition (London: Penguin, 2013).
Rodger, N. A. M., *The Safeguard of the sea: A naval history of Britain 660-1649*, Kindle edition (London: Penguin, 2004).
James, L., *The rise and fall of the British Empire*, new edition (London: Abacus, 1998).
Quinn, D. B., *Set fair for Roanoke: Voyages and colonies, 1584-1606*, (Chapel Hill and London: University of North Carolina Press, 1985).
Stick, D., *Roanoke Island: The beginnings of English America* (London: University of North Carolina Press, 1983).

[3] Sources:
Darwin, J., *Unfinished empire: The global expansion of Britain*, Penguin edition (London: Penguin, 2013).
James, L., *The rise and fall of the British Empire*, new edition (London: Abacus, 1998).
Rodger, N. A. M., *The Safeguard of the sea: A naval history of Britain 660-1649*, Kindle edition (London: Penguin, 2004).
Schama, S., *A history of Britain: At the edge of the world? 3000BC-AD1603*, Kindle edition (London: Bodley Head, 2009).
Stick, D., *Roanoke Island: The beginnings of English America* (London: University of North Carolina Press, 1983).

[4] Sources:
Appleby, J. C., 'War, politics and colonization, 1558-1625', in *The Oxford History of the British Empire: Volume 1, the origins of the empire, British overseas enterprise to the close of the seventeenth century*, ed. by N. Canny, 5 vols (Oxford: Oxford University Press, 1998), pp. 55-78.
Canny, N., 'England's new world and the old, 1480s-1630s', in *The Oxford History of the British Empire: Volume 1, the origins of the empire, British overseas enterprise to the close of the seventeenth century*, ed. by N. Canny, 5 vols (Oxford: Oxford University Press, 1998), pp. 148-168.
Darwin, J., *Unfinished empire: The global expansion of Britain*, Penguin edition (London: Penguin, 2013).
Ferguson, N., *Empire: How Britain made the modern world*, Penguin edition (London: Penguin, 2004).
Paxman, J., *Empire*, Penguin edition (London: Penguin, 2012).

[5] Sources:
Appleby, J. C., 'War, politics and colonization, 1558-1625', in *The Oxford History of the British Empire: Volume 1, the origins of the empire, British overseas*

enterprise to the close of the seventeenth century, ed. by N. Canny, 5 vols (Oxford: Oxford University Press, 1998), pp. 55-78.
Darwin, J., *Unfinished empire: The global expansion of Britain*, Penguin edition (London: Penguin, 2013).
James, L., *The rise and fall of the British Empire*, new edition (London: Abacus, 1998).
Perdue, T., and Green, M., *North American Indians: A very short introduction* (New York: Oxford University Press, 2010).

[6] Sources:
Guy, J., *The Tudors: A very short introduction*, 2nd edition (New York: Oxford University Press, 2013).
Morrill, J., *Stuart Britain: A very short introduction* (New York: Oxford University Press, 2000).
Schama, S., *A history of Britain: The British Wars 1603-1776*, Kindle edition (London: Bodley Head, 2009).
Tombs, R., *The English and their history* (London: Allen Lane, 2014).

[7] J. Darwin, *Unfinished empire: The global expansion of Britain*, Penguin edition (London: Penguin, 2013), p. xi; J. C. Appleby, 'War, politics and colonization, 1558-1625', in *The Oxford History of the British Empire: Volume 1, the origins of the empire, British overseas enterprise to the close of the seventeenth century*, ed. by N. Canny, 5 vols (Oxford: Oxford University Press, 1998), pp. 55-78.
(p. 64).
[8] N. Canny, 'England's new world and the old, 1480s-1630s', in *The Oxford History of the British Empire: Volume 1, the origins of the empire, British overseas enterprise to the close of the seventeenth century*, ed. by N. Canny, 5 vols (Oxford: Oxford University Press, 1998), pp. 148-168.
p. 150; N. Ferguson, *Empire: How Britain made the modern world*, Penguin edition (London: Penguin, 2004), p. 58.
[9] Darwin, *Unfinished Empire*, pp. 19, 36.
[10] J. Horn, 'Tobacco colonies: the shaping of English society in the Seventeenth-Century Chesapeake', in *The Oxford History of the British Empire: Volume 1, the origins of the empire, British overseas enterprise to the close of the seventeenth century*, ed. by N. Canny, 5 vols (Oxford: Oxford University Press, 1998), pp. 170-192, (p. 173).
[11] Darwin, Unfinished Empire, p. 36.
[12] Appleby, 'War, politics, colonisation', p. 68.
[13] Appleby, 'War, politics, colonisation', p. 70.
[14] Darwin, *Unfinished Empire*, p. 44.
[15] Horn, 'Tobacco colonies', p. 173.
[16] Appleby, 'War, politics, colonisation', p. 73; N. Dalziel, *The Penguin historical atlas of the British Empire* (London: penguin, 2006), p. 24; L. James,

The rise and fall of the British Empire, new edition (London: Abacus, 1998), p. 7.
[17] James, *Rise and fall*, p. 4.
[18] G. Chet, *The colonists' American Revolution: Preserving English liberty, 1607-1783* (Hoboken: Wiley Blackwell, 2020), p. 16; Dalziel, Historical atlas, p. 24; Darwin, *Unfinished Empire*, p. 44.
[19] Dalziel, *Historical atlas*, p. 24.
[20] Ferguson, *Empire*, p. 58.
[21] Appleby, 'War, politics, colonisation', p. 72; H. McD. Beckles, 'The "Hub of Empire": The Caribbean and Britain in the seventeenth century', in *The Oxford History of the British Empire: Volume 1, the origins of the empire, British overseas enterprise to the close of the seventeenth century*, ed. by N. Canny, 5 vols (Oxford: Oxford University Press, 1998), pp. 218-240, (p. 221).
[22] Beckles, 'Hub of empire', p. 221.
[23] Chet, *American Revolution*, p. 19.
[24] James, *Rise and fall*, pp. 10, 37.
[25] Beckles, 'Hub of empire', p. 222; J. Paxman, *Empire*, Penguin edition (London: Penguin, 2012), p. 30.
[26] Horn, 'Tobacco colonies', p. 174.
[27] James, *Rise and fall*, p. 8.
[28] Darwin, *Unfinished Empire*, pp. 18-19.
[29] Canny, 'England's new world', p. 151; Horn, 'Tobacco colonies', p. 154.
[30] Ferguson, *Empire*, p. 59.
[31] A. Pagden, 'The struggle for legitimacy and the image of empire in the Atlantic to c.1700', in *The Oxford History of the British Empire: Volume 1, the origins of the empire, British overseas enterprise to the close of the seventeenth century*, ed. by N. Canny, 5 vols (Oxford: Oxford University Press, 1998), pp. 34-54, (p. 34).
[32] Dalziel, *Historical atlas*, p. 24.
[33] Chet, *American Revolution*, p. 17.
[34] Beckles, 'Hub of empire', p. 220.
[35] 'Letters patent to Sir Thomas Gates and others', 10 April 1606, in P. Barbour, *The Jamestown voyages under the First Charter, 1606-1609*, (New York: Routledge, 2016), chapter 1; 'Instructions for government', 20 November 1606, in P. Barbour, *The Jamestown voyages under the First Charter, 1606-1609*, (New York: Routledge, 2016), chapter 1.
[36] S. Sarson, 'Introduction: Brief review of sources', in *The American Colonies and the British Empire, 1607-1783*, Part 1, vol. 1., 8 vols., Routledge edition, (New York: Routledge, 2016).
[37] Sarson, 'Introduction'.
[38] Dalziel, *Historical atlas*, p. 26.
[39] Chet, *American Revolution*, p. 18.
[40] S. Schama, *A history of Britain: The British Wars 1603-1776*, Kindle edition (London: Bodley Head, 2009), p. 102.

[41] J. Black, *The British Empire: A history and a debate*, (London: Routledge, 2015), p. 50.
[42] Black, *British Empire*, pp. 49-50; V. D. Anderson, 'New England in the seventeenth century', in *The Oxford History of the British Empire: Volume 1, the origins of the empire, British overseas enterprise to the close of the seventeenth century*, ed. by N. Canny, 5 vols (Oxford: Oxford University Press, 1998), pp. 193-216, (pp. 195-96).
[43] Anderson, 'New England', p. 193.
[44] Chet, *American Revolution*, p. 25; Dalziel, *Historical atlas*, p. 26.
[45] T. Hunt, *Ten cities that made an empire*, Penguin edition (London: Penguin, 2015), p. 25.
[46] Anderson, 'New England', pp. 196-98.

Chapter 7: England's Empire in Britain

Section 1: Introduction and Explanations

This chapter is a little different. So far in this book, we've taken quite a global approach. We've discussed England's early advances in the Atlantic and Asia and how these helped to lay the foundations for the later British Empire. Now it's time for us to start looking a bit more closely at Britain itself. What was going on at home in this period?

While I can't give you a complete overview of British history from the Middle Ages through to the early eighteenth century in one short chapter (at least, not without doing it really, really, badly), I can explain how the English came to dominate their neighbours, and the nation of Britain was formed.

You'll be relieved to know (or maybe disappointed) that there aren't quite so many explanations in this chapter. However, since we'll be covering a period that we haven't touched on yet, there are still a few. First, we'll look at two of the most important English Kings, Edward I and Henry II. They both played pivotal roles in the gradual unification of the British Isles, and we must pay some attention to them. After that, I'll talk briefly about the English Reformation, which had a massive effect on British society.

Who was Edward I?

Edward I was the first King of England after the Norman Conquest in 1066 to have an English name instead of a French one. He was born in 1239 and grew to over 6 feet tall. This was massive for the time and earned him his nickname 'longshanks'.

He had a very active youth, going to Gascony in 1252 to secure the loyalty of the local elite on behalf of his father. He competed in his first tournament in 1256 before going on a family pilgrimage in Scotland. Civil war ravaged the reign of his father, Henry III, and Edward's military prowess was pivotal in helping Henry retain the throne. After doing this, Edward decided to go on a crusade to the Near East. He had trouble securing funds, which encouraged him to introduce measures to persecute English Jews to help raise money.

In 1272 he was in Sicily returning from his trip when he heard that his father had died and he had been proclaimed king. Despite this, he did not rush back to England. Instead, he stayed in France for a time, only returning to England in 1274.

Edward ruled in a period of growth and increasing commercialisation. He was determined to put the funds this gave him to use. First, he attacked Wales, initially only planning to change its ruler, before a rebellion convinced him to conquer the whole country and take direct control. After this, he turned his gaze towards Scotland and betrothed his son to the six-year-old heir to the Scottish throne. Soon after this, her grandfather, the king, died. When she also died, Edward asserted that he had the right to choose the next king. He became more aggressively involved in Scottish politics, eventually resulting in armed conflict that led to the Latin inscription on his tomb reading 'here lies the hammer of the Scots'.

Edward was more than just a military leader. He also implemented many new laws regarding the rights of the king and his subjects. He died in 1307 and is often remembered as one of England's most successful Medieval rulers.[1]

Who was Henry II?

Henry II of England grew up in a tumultuous time. His mother, daughter of King Henry I, was locked in a civil war with William the Conqueror's grandson Stephen over who would wear the crown. They eventually solved the despite with the compromise that Stephen would be king, but Henry would be his heir.

Henry was a strong, brave, and courageous man with a fiery temper. He inherited a massive empire stretching from the Scottish border to southern France and spent his life travelling around his land trying to secure it. This was far from an easy task. Many rebel baronies rose in the chaos preceding his reign, which Henry crushed. He also humiliated the King of Scotland and became involved in Irish politics.

But Henry was more than just a military leader. He introduced many legal reforms that strengthened the bonds between the ruler and his subjects, and under him, land seizures from barons became more common.

Despite all this, Henry's reign had its troubles. He is perhaps most remembered for the murder of the Archbishop of Canterbury, Thomas Beckett. It is unclear whether the knights who killed Beckett acted on orders from the king, but Henry's arguments with Beckett are well documented. It is no stretch to believe that Henry (and many other influential people in England) wanted Beckett dead, even if he did not order it explicitly.

However, it was not the killing of Beckett that was to end his reign. As a young man aged 18, he married the 30-year-old Eleanor of Aquitane. At first, they seemed to have genuine feelings for one another, but later in life, cracks appeared in the marriage. Henry had his wife imprisoned. This led to clashes with his children, most notably her favourite, the future Richard I (whose fame as 'Richard the Lionheart' often overshadows his father). Henry made this rift worse by trying to take land from Richard to give to another of his sons, John. After this, Richard, with support from King Philip of France, fought and humiliated his father. Henry II died a few weeks later.[2]

What was the English Reformation?

Europe went through a dramatic shift in the sixteenth century. The rise of the printing press allowed Martin Luther (and others) to spread the idea that the Catholic Church was insufficient and that people needed a more direct relationship with God. They wanted to print Bibles in English, French, and other vernacular languages rather than just Latin, as was the norm.

Initially, the Reformation struggled to find royal support in England. Henry VIII didn't find the idea enticing, and the vast majority of the population was quite content with the Catholic Church. However, things changed when Henry wanted to divorce his first wife, Katherine of Aragon. The Pope would not allow it, so Henry decided to break from the Catholic Church and declare himself the head of the new Church of England. He even made it treason for anyone to dispute his right to be head of the Church.

Henry dissolved the monasteries and plundered them to boost his royal treasury. He also attacked traditional church holidays, which did not go down well with the country's rural population. The reformation thus introduced social and political changes as well as religious ones. It had dramatic and long-lasting effects on the formation of the British state and relationships with other countries, such as Ireland.

Henry was the first European king to break from the Catholic Church, and his changes were not set in stone. Under his children, the situation fluctuated wildly. His son, Edward, was very Protestant, but his daughter Mary was very Catholic and undid some reforms. However, his second daughter, Elizabeth, firmly established Protestantism as the main religion in England.[3]

Section 2: The British Isles as an Empire

In the *Penguin Atlas of the British Empire,* Nigel Dalziel argues that at the same time as creating a global empire, England was forming a regional empire in the British Isles.[4] Whether the other countries in the British Isles should be considered 'colonies' has been the topic of debate.[5] However, what is undoubtedly clear is that by 1707, Britain had formed into a relatively cohesive unit. This chapter will look at how this happened.

Wales

Until the twentieth century, people didn't often discuss the idea of Wales being an English colony.[6] This is surprising. There were many signs during the English invasion that they were attempting to colonise Wales, such as the attempts to settle communities of English peasants on Welsh land.[7]

Edward I introduced a variety of measures to control Wales after his victory in 1283. He attacked indigenous Welsh culture and placed legal restrictions on the activities of the Welsh people.[8] He also destroyed the Welsh ruling dynasties and introduced English methods of governance and law.[9] In another effort to control the country, Edward took personal ownership of large swathes of land.[10] Many aristocrats lost their holdings, although the king did reward those lords who had been loyal to him with land or victory in their local power struggles.[11]

Despite all this, Edward's attempts were not entirely successful. In the reign of his son, Wales was still not fully integrated into England.[12] The country was fractured, and many different factions were involved in its governance.[13] Many lords used the chaos caused by this fragmentation to retain some degree of independence and autonomy, helping Wales to maintain an identity separate from England.[14]

By the mid-sixteenth century, Wales had become more fully integrated into the English Parliament and system of administration.[15] Thus, by our study period, Wales was entirely a part of 'Britain' as a political body, rather than just a geographical area. However, the earlier period of fractures and factionalism as Wales resisted Edward I's attempts at cultural erasure had a lasting impact. The fact that Wales retained its own identity, despite being under English rule allows us to consider whether we should view it as a colony.

Scotland

After the death of Elizabeth I, King James VI of Scotland became James I of England. It would be natural to assume that the placement of a Scottish King on the English throne would quickly bring the countries into a close union. This did not happen.

The Stuart Kings (James' family) struggled to build closer ties between the two lands. The rarity with which they visited Scotland, and England's place as the decision-making hub, caused resentment among Scots.[16] This was troubling, as relations between the two countries were already strained due to anger at the way in which Oliver Cromwell annexed Scotland during his Protectorate.[17] Likewise, even with a Scottish king on the throne, the English Parliament was not convinced that a political union between the two countries was a good idea.[18]

Over time, however, the Scots became convinced that a union with England was a necessary evil. Firstly, having their king as an absentee ruler living in England but still making critical decisions about Scotland became increasingly problematic.[19] Similarly, the failure of Scottish attempts to create overseas colonies drove them closer to England.[20] In short, by the time of the Act of Union in 1707, many Scots felt they had no choice.

The union was far from equally balanced. England's population was several times that of Scotland, and they were the dominant partner in the relationship.[21] Despite this, the union did not wholly destroy the Scottish political systems; neither did it disenfranchise the Scottish people, as they could still vote for members of parliament.[22]

The expansion of Britain's empire was pivotal for the union's success as it gave many Scots a stake in 'Britain'.[23] Many Scottish people would play essential roles in the imperial administration.[24] In short, England and Scotland were tied together by the chance to mutually benefit from an empire, as well as the political reality of England's dominance.

Ireland

England's expansion into Ireland began with the Norman kings and their efforts at colonisation.[25] They exploited local divisions. Henry II was first invited into the country as part of a regional power struggle.[26] Over the coming centuries, England would gradually increase its holdings and influence.[27]

England's position weakened when Henry VIII converted the country to Protestantism. Their authority had come from the Pope's agreement that Britain should govern Ireland. With England breaking from the Catholic Church, this became irrelevant.[28]

England resorted to force. After the chaos of the English Civil War, Oliver Cromwell launched a crushing and brutal attack on Ireland.[29] Later in the century, when the Protestant William of Orange deposed the Catholic James II and was offered the English throne by parliament, Ireland stayed loyal to James and became embroiled in a war.[30] By the end of this war, the Catholic leadership of Ireland had largely been killed or exiled. The few who remained generally supported the Protestant regime.[31] Cromwell's victory had established English Protestant dominance over the predominantly Catholic Irish, and William guaranteed this state of affairs would continue for the foreseeable future.[32]

Catholic landholding was reduced, and a series of wide-ranging property laws restricted Catholic life, even down the value of a horse they could own.[33] Perhaps most crushingly of all, Catholics were excluded from the Dublin-based parliament, meaning that the descendants of previous English Protestant colonists dominated the government.[34]

Across the eighteenth century, some of these restrictions did ease.[35] Although, when Britain achieved a formal union with Ireland in 1800, allegations of corruption were rife.[36] This suggests that even then, Ireland was a junior partner being dominated and abused by the rest of Britain.

Historians disagree over whether Ireland was a colony between the sixteenth and eighteenth centuries.[37] But there can be no doubt that England had achieved a high level of dominance over Ireland by the early eighteenth century. This ensured their predominance in the British Isles, allowing them to set their sights further afield towards creating a global British Empire.

Lessons from the formation of Britain

Although there is debate over the extent to which countries like Ireland and Wales were colonies, by the definition of imperialism that we discussed in part one, England's actions in driving the formation of Britain were acts of imperialism. England repeated its tactics time and again across the world. Thus, whether we consider the formation of Britain as the creation of an empire or not, it was undoubtedly the creation of an imperialist.

---

[1] Sources:
Davies, S., *Edward I's conquest of Wales* (Barnsley; Pen and Sword, 2017).
Gillingham, J., and Griffiths, R. A., *Medieval Britain: A very short introduction*, (New York: Oxford University Press, 2000).

King, A., and Spencer, A. M., 'Introduction', in *Edward I: New interpretations*, ed. by A. King and A. M. Spencer, (Rochester: York Medieval Press, 2020), pp. 1-8.
Schama, S., *A history of Britain: At the edge of the world? 3000BC-AD1603*, Kindle edition (London: Bodley Head, 2009).
Tombs, R., *The English and their history* (London: Allen Lane, 2014).

[2] Sources:
Asbridge, T., *The Greatest Knight: The remarkable life of William Marshall, the power behind five English thrones*, (London: Simon and Schuster, 2015).
Gillingham, J., and Griffiths, R. A., *Medieval Britain: A very short introduction*, (New York: Oxford University Press, 2000).
Schama, S., *A history of Britain: At the edge of the world? 3000BC-AD1603*, Kindle edition (London: Bodley Head, 2009).
Tombs, R., *The English and their history* (London: Allen Lane, 2014).
Turner, R. V., and Heiser, R., *The reign of Richard Lionheart: Ruler of the Angevin Empire, 1189-1199*, Routledge edition (Abingdon: Routledge, 2013).

[3] Sources:
Guy, J., *The Tudors: A very short introduction*, 2nd edition (New York: Oxford University Press, 2013).
Ryrie, A., *The English reformation: A very brief history* (London: SPCK, 2020).
Schama, S., *A history of Britain: At the edge of the world? 3000BC-AD1603*, Kindle edition (London: Bodley Head, 2009).
Tombs, R., *The English and their history* (London: Allen Lane, 2014).
Wood, M., *The story of England*, Kindle edition (London: Viking, 2010).

[4] N. Dalziel, *The Penguin historical atlas of the British Empire* (London: Penguin, 2006), p. 8.
[5] R. R. Davies, 'Colonial Wales', *Past and Present*, 65 (1974), 3-23, (pp. 3-4); J. Gibney, *A short history of Ireland* (New Haven and London: Yale University Press, 2017), (pp. 85-86).
[6] Davies, 'Colonial Wales', p. 3.
[7] Davies, 'Colonial Wales', pp. 3-4; S. Davies, *Edward I's conquest of Wales* (Barnsley; Pen and Sword, 2017), chapter 10.
[8] S. Schama, *A history of Britain: At the edge of the world? 3000BC-AD1603*, Kindle edition (London: Bodley Head, 2009), pp. 185-87.
[9] M. Prestwich, 'Edward I and Wales', in *The impact of the Edwardian castles in Wales: The proceedings of a conference held at Bangor University, 7-9 September 2007*, ed. by D. M. Williams and J. R. Kenyon (Oxford: Oxbow books, 2010), pp. 1-8, (p. 1).
[10] S Davies, *Conquest*, chapter 10.
[11] Davies, *Conquest*, chapter 10.

[12] R. R. Davies, *The age of conquest: Wales 1063-1415*, 2nd edition, (New York: Oxford University Press, 2000), p. 391.
[13] Davies, *Age of conquest*, pp. 391-92.
[14] Davies, *Age of conquest*, p. 391.
[15] A. I. Macinnes, *Union and Empire: The making of the United Kingdom in 1707*, (New York: Cambridge University Press, 2007), p. 4.
[16] D. Allan, *Scotland in the eighteenth Century: Union and enlightenment*, Routledge edition (Abingdon: Routledge, 2013), chapter 1.
[17] T. M. Devine, '300 years of the Anglo-Scottish Union', in *Scotland and the Union, 1707-2007*, ed. by T. M. Devine (Edinburgh: Edinburgh University press, 2008), pp. 1-19, p. 3.
[18] Macinnes, *Union and empire*, p. 4.
[19] Allan, *Scotland*, chapter 1.
[20] S. Schama, *A history of Britain: The British Wars 1603-1776*, Kindle edition (London: Bodley Head, 2009), pp. 335-37.
[21] Devine, '300 years', p. 1; Macinnes, *Union and empire*, pp. 3-11, 313-26.
[22] Schama, *The British wars*, p. 340.
[23] Macinnes, *Union and empire*, p. 6.
[24] J. Darwin, *Unfinished empire: The global expansion of Britain*, Penguin edition (London: Penguin, 2013), p. 294; Schama, *The British wars*, chapter 5.
[25] Gibney, *Short history*, p. 6.
[26] C. Veach, 'Conquest and conquerors', in *The Cambridge History of Ireland: Volume 1, 600-1500*, ed. by B. Smith, 4 vols., (Cambridge: Cambridge University Press, 2018), pp. 157-182, (pp. 157-58).
[27] Veach, 'Conquest and conquerors'.
[28] Gibney, *Short history*, pp. 15-16.
[29] Gibney, *Short history*, p. 68.
[30] F. O'Gorman, *The long eighteenth century: British political and social history, 1688-1832*, 2nd edition (London: Bloomsbury, 2016); C. I. McGrath, 'Politics, 1692-1730', in *The Cambridge history of Ireland. Volume II, 1550-1730*, ed. by J. Ohlmeyer, 4 vols., (Cambridge: Cambridge University Press, 2018), pp. 120-143, (p. 120).
[31] D. W. Hayton, 'The emergence of a Protestant society, 1691-1730', in *The Cambridge history of Ireland. Volume II, 1550-1730*, ed. by J. Ohlmeyer, 4 vols., (Cambridge: Cambridge University Press, 2018), p. 144-168, (pp. 144-45).
[32] J. Gibney, 'Introduction: Rebellions and Union', in *The United Irishmen, rebellion and the Act of Union, 1791-1803*, ed. by J. Gibney (Philadelphia: Pen and Sword, 2018); Hayton, 'Emergence', p. 144.
[33] Hayton, 'Emergence', p. 147; McGrath, 'Politics', p. 123.
[34] Gibney, 'Introduction: Rebellions and Union'; Hayton, 'Emergence', p. 147.
[35] Gibney, 'Introduction: Rebellions and Union'.

[36] P. M. Geoghegan, '"An act of power and corruption"? The Union debate', in *The United Irishmen, rebellion and the Act of Union, 1791-1803*, ed. by J. Gibney (Philadelphia: Pen and Sword, 2018).
[37] Gibney, *Short history*, pp. 85-86.

Chapter 8: War

Section 1: Introduction and Explanations

The next chapter is about how England's wars in the seventeenth century helped to grow the British Empire. I've spent a lot of time in this book talking about the actions of individuals or relatively peaceful trade, but large-scale warfare between states was also a crucial part of the birth of the British Empire.

There are four explanations this time. The first provides some context on the English Civil Wars. These wars make up a large part of this chapter, and it is essential that you know a little about the conflicts to make sense of my analysis. Similarly, there's an explanation of the Restoration, discussing how the Stuart family later returned to the English throne.

Of course, the Civil Wars and the Restoration are quite well-known areas of history (within England at least), so you may already know a fair bit about them. The other two explanations are a little more niche.

One discusses the Dutch Empire, a significant early rival to the British. The Dutch were closely linked to England in the seventeenth century, both as allies and enemies, so it is important to know how they operated. Along these lines, you may also want to remind yourself about the Glorious Revolution, as this event involving England and the Dutch will be very important in this chapter.

The final explanation is the most complicated of the three and the one you are least likely to be familiar with. It breaks down the concept of the 'fiscal-military state', which is an incredibly useful way of understanding the changes in government at the end of the seventeenth century.

What were the English Civil Wars?

In the middle of the seventeenth century, a variety of religious, political, and economic problems dragged England into civil war. The English financial system was weak, and the King's powers were unclear due to the lack of a written constitution. Conflicts with Ireland and Scotland caused many issues for King Charles I and increased tensions between him and his parliament. Parliament believed that Charles was abusing his power, taxing people beyond his rights, and enforcing a dangerously Catholic form of religion, which the mainly Protestant gentry disliked. Which of these many problems caused the first Civil War is the subject of widespread debate, but whatever the reason, by 1642, Charles I and his parliament were raising troops to fight each other.

At first, Charles' resources seemed pitiful when compared to parliament's. But he quickly changed this, and by the Battle of Edgehill (the first major battle of the war), his troops outnumbered the parliamentarians. Things seemed to be going well for Charles and the Royalists. However, their undisciplined troops meant that they failed to capitalise on their successes.

Over time, the war swung decisively in parliament's favour. They created the highly professional New Model Army and allied with the Scots. Following the Battle of Naseby in 1645, parliament's victory was only a matter of time. They had almost entirely destroyed Charles' army and went on to win the first war.

As peace settlements were ongoing, Charles escaped his parliamentarian captors and formed a new alliance with the Scots. This resulted in the start of a new war.

The Second Civil War was brief, and parliament quickly defeated Charles and his new allies. Following this, the army seized Charles and purged parliament of its more moderate members. They executed Charles, leaving the country in the hands of religious extremists who would rule until the Restoration of Charles II in 1660.[1]

What was the Restoration?

Following Charles I's execution during the English Civil Wars came a period where England was a Commonwealth, governed by Oliver Cromwell as Lord Protector. In 1660, after Cromwell's death, Charles II, son of Charles I, was offered the throne. This event is known as the 'Restoration', as the monarchy was 'restored'.

What came next was a significant shift in the day-to-day life in the country. Most of the people were very happy with parliament giving Charles the throne. In contrast to the austere years of the Commonwealth, he held a lavish court and was a notorious pleasure seeker with many illegitimate children. All acts of parliament since Charles I's execution were declared void, and the flagship of the fleet, the *Naseby*, was even renamed the *Royal Charles*.

Surprisingly, Charles II was relatively lenient to his former political rivals. He agreed not to prosecute the vast majority, although he had Oliver Cromwell's remains dug up and the corpse hanged. Charles also tried to include former parliamentarians in official positions in his new regime. However, many Royalist officials were not so forgiving and gleefully persecuted their parliamentarian rivals. This quest for revenge wasn't just limited to officials. People of all social classes took the opportunity to get revenge on Puritan priests that had spent the last decade in power.[2]

What was the Dutch Empire?

The Dutch Empire was based on trade and commerce rather than colonisation. After fighting a long series of wars to gain their independence from Spain, the Dutch Republic put the financial experience they had gained to good use. They began by supporting the Spanish and Portuguese Empires in the Atlantic before forming the VOC (Dutch East India Company) to challenge Portugal's dominant role in European trade with East Asia. Fears over the potential of Dutch success helped to inspire the English East India Company, although the starting funds for the VOC were several times that of the British.

As with the British Empire, the nature of the Dutch Empire varied a little depending on the place. In Japan, Dutch merchants were much less powerful than the authorities. However, they became dominant in Indonesia and seized control of the spice trade.

In general, the Dutch had fewer formal colonies than other European empires. They succeeded by becoming reliable merchants who always paid their debts. This made bankers more willing to loan them the funds they needed to expand commerce and build armies.

They played a pivotal role in transporting goods to and from the colonies of these other European powers. In the first half of the sixteenth century, the Dutch were significant players in both the spice and sugar industries, and the value of their overseas trade was at least double that of England.

When they did conquer a region, the Dutch didn't try to assimilate indigenous people into their culture. Instead, they left them mainly to govern themselves. However, we should be cautious in viewing the Dutch form of imperialism as more benevolent than the British. Their colonies in Asia relied on slave labour, and the Dutch were perfectly capable of genocide when it suited their needs.[3]

What is the fiscal-military state?

The fiscal-military state is a concept developed by John Brewer to explain how Britain changed from a minor power in the sixteenth and seventeenth-century European wars to a major power in the late seventeenth and early eighteenth centuries. Building on work that noted the higher rate of taxation on British citizens as opposed to French, Brewer argued that the political crises Britain faced in the seventeenth century created a government that wielded limited powers very effectively to raise taxes in order to fund a military. This, in turn, created a 'financial community' that has strong influences on politics and economics to this day.

Many historians have since developed this theory further, for example, by extending it to other countries, like the Dutch Republic. Some have also looked more closely at the precise details of the fiscal-military state and how it changed over time or how the fiscal-military state's high taxation helped fund government borrowing. A more recent trend is to focus on how the state spent the money it raised, such as on mercenaries or private contracts, giving birth to the concept of the 'contractor state'.[4]

Section 2: The Seventeenth-Century Wars and the British Empire

Across the seventeenth century, a variety of conflicts increased English, and later British, power. In some cases, it's pretty easy to see how this worked. For example, Cromwell and the Stuart kings used military force to conquer colonies and seize control of trade. In other instances, when economic gains are less obvious, we must look a little deeper and see how these wars helped to shape the fledgling British state.

The English Civil Wars

You could be forgiven for wondering how a conflict in which Englishmen killed each other could possibly have helped to advance Britain's global position. However, developments during and after the Civil Wars were crucial to Britain's later success.

One way we can see this is by studying the strengthening of the British armed forces. On land, this meant the creation of the New Model Army. The New Model Army was a professional army created by merging existing units and funded through regular taxation.[5] Unlike the other armies of the Civil Wars, it was a national army, not tied to any local region.[6] It was trained to be very disciplined and opened up the rank of officer to a much more comprehensive range of society.[7] In many ways, the New Model Army foreshadowed what the British army would become in later centuries.

Now, we mustn't get carried away here. The New Model Army did not lead directly to the armies of the Napoleonic Wars; Charles II abolished it during the Restoration.[8] However, it certainly had a significant impact on Britain in the immediate aftermath of the Civil Wars.

The navy also changed dramatically as a result of the conflict. Sailors at this time were more politically moderate than soldiers, and many deserted after the execution of King

Charles I.[9] Therefore, despite parliament's victory providing the funds to maintain a modern military, the navy was left crippled by internal divisions.[10] Nevertheless, those in power following the Civil Wars were religious extremists who idolised figures such as Francis Drake and believed in the power of a strong navy. As such, they were more than willing to commit to rebuilding it.[11]

Political fallout from the Civil Wars

This brings me to my next point. The political changes in England resulting from the Civil Wars were crucial to the development of the British Empire. After executing their king, the English Parliament faced enemies on all sides, and their policies reflected this.[12] They immediately moved to strengthen their position both financially and militarily. The Civil Wars and the following shift to a military dictatorship helped create Britain's tax state, the fiscal-military state.[13]

More specifically, it was then that parliament introduced the first Navigation Act. This helped strengthen Britain's position against rivals such as the Dutch and made England's colonies subject to parliament.[14] The Navigation Act was part of a process where chartered companies and state-granted monopolies began to decrease in power and number. Instead, the English people more broadly (those wealthy enough to be involved in trade, at least) started to reap the rewards of imperialism.[15] In short, the English Civil Wars led to financial developments that played a crucial role in creating the individualistic form of the British Empire.

Cromwell's Wars

After the Civil Wars, Oliver Cromwell increasingly dominated English politics and led England in several wars.

Ireland and Scotland

First, Cromwell led English troops against Ireland and Scotland, bringing them under English military rule.[16] This was nothing particularly new. Parliament had been trying to get Ireland under control since 1642, when the 'Adventurer's Act' was passed. This act promised the land of Irish rebels to those who would fund its conquest.[17] However, the brutality of Cromwell's actions, including a massacre at Drogheda, went far beyond these earlier attempts at suppression and would damage Anglo-Irish relations for centuries.[18]

The First Anglo-Dutch War

Although it may not have the same place in the public mind as the Napoleonic Wars, the First Anglo-Dutch War had a considerable impact on the early growth of the British Empire.[19] It was a war with a dual purpose. Firstly, alongside the Navigation Act, it expanded English trade at the expense of the Dutch, who were a significant rival to England.[20] This helped to improve England's global trade power, as did the 1654 Treaty of Westminster, which ended the war and forced the Dutch to accept the Navigation Act.[21] Capturing 1700 ships during the war also gave English merchants the means to carry all the goods that the Navigation Act required.[22]

However, the First Anglo-Dutch War was not entirely about trade. Those politicians who decided to go to war were not acting under any pressure from merchants. They were more concerned about the national security threat posed by the strong Dutch navy and its ties to the deposed Stuart family.[23] In this sense, the war was about defending the newly formed republic. As such, it contributed to the modernisation of England's navy, as it moved away from a wartime fleet of hired vessels and towards becoming a professional force.[24]

International Reputation

This strengthening of England's military under Cromwell brought international prestige and territorial gains.[25] In addition to unifying Britain, Cromwell allied with France against the Spanish to win land in the New World.[26] The war with Spain was a military success, resulting in the capture of

Jamaica, a Spanish treasure fleet worth over £2,000,000 (a massive amount at the time), and the port of Dunkirk, which had long been a base for Spanish privateers.[27] However, this victory came at a cost. Despite England's military reputation being higher than ever, Cromwell's wars left the military in crippling debt.[28]

The Later Stuarts

The English military had mixed fortunes under the reign of the restored Charles II and his successor James II. Charles inherited an army and navy in significant debt and had to move quickly to fix this growing problem.[29] He thus disbanded the New Model Army, although he committed to retaining a strong navy.[30] In the short term, this did not go well. Throughout the early years of his reign, the navy was corrupt and inefficient.[31]

A group of ministers led by James, Charles' brother and heir, incited the Second Anglo-Dutch War, hoping to increase royal authority.[32] It ended badly, and the English suffered a defeat. However, the Dutch terms were relatively mild, allowing the English to keep several of the colonial gains they had recently made, including key locations such as New York and Cape Coast Castle.[33]

Over time, the situation improved, and the later Stuarts sowed the seeds for imperial success. Some of the reforms brought in by Charles to pay off Cromwell's naval debts helped to increase trade and shipping.[34] Both Charles and James were very interested in the navy, which many in England came to see as the 'physical embodiment of England's political and religious freedom'.[35] Charles even convinced parliament to increase taxes to fund the navy so it could meet France's growing power.[36]

Over the course of the seventeenth century, the state gained greater control over sea power, making the navy more suitable to protect a global empire rather than just defending

England.[37] By the time of the Third Anglo-Dutch War (again inspired by the selfish motives of officers and politicians), England was able to perform much better as a military power.[38]

The Glorious Revolution

You may be surprised that I have included the Glorious Revolution here; many people have viewed it as a relatively peaceful transition of power.[39] However, it undoubtedly existed in a military context and was tied deeply to ongoing military conflicts in Europe.

Many feared that when he became king, Charles's brother, the future James II, would ally himself with the warmongering Louis XIV of France.[40] However, Louis was complacent over the threat faced by his friend James and believed that an invasion of England would be doomed to fail. He, therefore, sent his fleet to the Mediterranean and his army to Germany. This took pressure off the Dutch Republic and freed up the troops that William of Orange needed to invade England.[41]

The Dutch were prepared for a fight; their invasion fleet was around four times the size of the Spanish Armada.[42] James did not intend to surrender peacefully either. He had a larger army than William, although it was inexperienced and scattered around the country.[43] Despite this, he commanded the population of Britain to arm themselves and resist William.[44] Although riots in London limited the number of troops he could spare, James also sent part of his army to block William's approach to the capital.[45]

However, James' commanders, including Edward Hyde, Earl of Clarendon, a loyal Royalist throughout the Civil Wars, and John Churchill, the future Duke of Marlborough (a famous British military leader), deserted him and switched sides.[46] Ultimately, James fled the country.[47]

Although the transition of power in England may have been relatively peaceful, we should not downplay the military aspects of the Revolution.[48] It started conflicts in Scotland and Ireland in which many lost their lives.[49] Likewise, a few members of parliament may well have invited William to the country, but making himself king went far beyond what they had intended. In short, he used his military power to take what he wanted.[50]

William's intentions for England are the most crucial evidence that the Glorious Revolution was an important military event for Britain. The Dutch would have been vulnerable to a combined attack by the French and English. As such, William took the English throne and brought the country into the European struggle against Louis XIV's France.[51] This, combined with James having fled and sought help from Louis, increased the tensions between England and France and seriously weakened the latter's international position.[52]

The Glorious Revolution was, therefore, a military event inspired by an international war. The military aspects of it shaped British foreign policy for the next century as Britain clashed again and again with France.[53]

Steady progress across the century

These conflicts helped the English (soon to be British) Empire to develop steadily throughout the seventeenth century. The Royal Navy gradually became more professional, helping England defend its growing international trade.[54] This proved especially important later in the century, given that the Glorious Revolution brought England into a major global conflict; a strong navy would be crucial.[55] The idea that the British Empire was an 'empire of the seas' would remain central in British ideology for centuries to come.[56]

Even beyond the armed forces, these conflicts changed England both within and without. In terms of culture and society, the rise of individual liberties in this period helped to transform England into a global power and shaped the individualistic and varied nature of the British Empire.[57]

Likewise, the steady weakening of the Dutch Empire aided the rise of Britain's empire. Paul Kennedy has argued against the idea that the British Empire sprang from the ashes of the Dutch, believing instead that the British success came from accessing new markets.[58] This may be entirely true, but the Dutch Empire was a rival, and anything Britain won from them helped the empire to grow.[59] The spoils of their wars included key locations in America and Africa that shaped the character of the British Empire in the eighteenth century.[60]

Considering everything we have studied in this chapter, it is clear that across the seventeenth century, Britain's power in Europe and the world increased through military victories and the strengthening of the armed forces. Britain changed dramatically during this time, and its rising power respective to its European rivals would only continue in the eighteenth and nineteenth centuries.

---

[1] Sources:
Bennet, M., *The English Civil War, 1640-1649*, new edition (Abingdon: Routledge, 2013).
Gaunt, P., *The English Civil War: A military history* (New York: I.B. Tauris, 2014).
Purkiss, D., *The English Civil War: A people's history*, Harper Perennial edition (London: Harper Perennial, 2010).
Roberts, C., Roberts, F. D., and Bisson, D., *A history of England: Volume 1*, 2 vols., 2nd edition (New York: Routledge, 2016).
Schama, S., *A history of Britain: The British Wars 1603-1776*, Kindle edition (London: Bodley Head, 2009).
Tombs, R., *The English and their history* (London: Allen Lane, 2014).

[2] Sources:
Miller, J., *The Restoration and the England of Charles II*, Routledge edition (Abingdon: Routledge, 2014).
Morrill, J., *Stuart Britain: A very short introduction* (New York: Oxford University Press, 2000).

Schama, S., *A history of Britain: The British Wars 1603-1776*, Kindle edition (London: Bodley Head, 2009).
Tombs, R., *The English and their history*, (London: Allen Lane, 2014).
Wood, M., *The story of England*, Kindle edition (London: Viking, 2010).

[3] Sources:
Antunes, C. 'Introduction', in *Exploring the Dutch Empire: Agents, networks and institutions, 1600-2000*, ed. by C Antunes and J. Gommans (London: Bloomsbury, 2015).
Clulow, A., and Mostert, T., 'Introduction: The companies in Asia', in *The Dutch and English East India Companies: Diplomacy, trade and violence in early modern Asia*, ed. by A. Clulow and T. Mostert (Amsterdam: Amsterdam University Press, 2018), pp. 13-21.
Gommans, J., 'Conclusion: Globalizing empire: The Dutch case', in *Exploring the Dutch Empire: Agents, networks and institutions, 1600-2000*, ed. by C Antunes and J. Gommans (London: Bloomsbury, 2015).
Harari, Y. N., *Sapiens: A brief history of humankind* (London: Vintage, 2011).
Koot, C. J., *Empire at the periphery: British colonists, Anglo-Dutch trade and the development of the British Atlantic, 1621-1713* (London: New York University Press, 2011).
Odegard, E., 'Merchant companies at war: The Anglo-Dutch wars in Asia', in *War, trade and the state: Anglo-Dutch conflict, 1652-88*, ed. by D. Ormrod and G. Rommelse, (Woodbridge: The Boydell Press, 2020), pp. 230-247.
Ormrod, D., and Rommelse, G., 'Introduction: Anglo-Dutch conflict in the North Sea and beyond', in *War, trade and the state: Anglo-Dutch conflict, 1652-88*, ed. by D. Ormrod and G. Rommelse, (Woodbridge: The Boydell Press, 2020), pp. 3-33.

[4] Sources:
Bowen, H. V. et. al., 'Forum: The contractor state c. 1650-1815', *International Journal of Maritime History*, 25.1 (2013), 239-274.
Brewer, J. *The sinews of power: War, money and the English state, 1688-1783*, e-library edition (London: Taylor and Francis, 2005).
Graham. A., and Walsh, P., 'Introduction', in *The British fiscal-military states, 1660-c.1783*, ed. by A. Graham and P. Walsh (Abingdon: Routledge, 2016).
Ormrod, D., and Rommelse, G., 'Introduction: Anglo-Dutch conflict in the North Sea and beyond', in *War, trade and the state: Anglo-Dutch conflict, 1652-88*, ed. by D. Ormrod and G. Rommelse (Woodbridge: The Boydell Press, 2020), pp. 3-33.
Stone, L., 'Introduction', in *An imperial state at war: Britain from 1689-1815*, ed. by L. Stone (Abingdon: Routledge, 1994).

Storrs, C., 'Introduction: The fiscal-military state in the 'long' eighteenth century' in *The fiscal-military state in eighteenth-century Europe: Essays in honour of P. G. M. Dickinson*, ed. by C. Storrs, Routledge edition (Abingdon: Routledge, 2016).

[5] C. Roberts, F. D. Roberts, and D. Bisson, *A history of England: Volume 1*, 2 vols., 2nd edition (New York: Routledge, 2016), chapter 14; M., Bennet, *The English Civil War, 1640-1649*, new edition (Abingdon: Routledge, 2013), chapter 10.
[6] Roberts, Roberts, and Bisson, *History of England*, chapter 14.
[7] S. Schama, *A history of Britain: The British Wars 1603-1776*, Kindle edition (London: Bodley Head, 2009), chapter 2.
[8] P. Gaunt, *The English Civil War: A military history* (New York: I.B. Tauris, 2014), pp. 248-49.
[9] N. A. M. Rodger, *The command of the ocean: A naval history of Britain, 1649-1815*, new edition (London: Penguin, 2006), p. 2.
[10] N. A. M. Rodger, *The Safeguard of the sea: A naval history of Britain 660-1649*, Kindle edition (London: Penguin, 2004), pp. 424-46.
[11] P. Kennedy, *The rise and fall of British naval mastery*, new edition (London: Penguin, 2017), p. 45.
[12] Rodger, *Safeguard of the sea*, p. 426.
[13] D. Ormrod, and G. Rommelse, 'Introduction: Anglo-Dutch conflict in the North Sea and beyond', in *War, trade and the state: Anglo-Dutch conflict, 1652-88*, ed. by D. Ormrod and G. Rommelse, (Woodbridge: The Boydell Press, 2020), pp. 3-33, (p. 21).
[14] Ormrod and Rommelse, 'Introduction', p. 10; Roberts, Roberts, and Bisson, *History of England*, chapter 14; Kennedy, *British naval mastery*, p. 46.
[15] Kennedy, *British naval mastery*, p. 47.
[16] Gaunt, *The English Civil War*, p. 245.
[17] Roberts, Roberts, and Bisson, *History of England*, chapter 14.
[18] Schama, *The British Wars*, chapter 3.
[19] J. R. Jones, *The Anglo-Dutch wars of the seventeenth century* (Abingdon: Routledge, 1996), introduction.
[20] J. Darwin, *Unfinished empire: The global expansion of Britain*, Penguin edition (London: Penguin, 2013), p. 10; Jones, *Anglo-Dutch Wars*, introduction; Kennedy, *British naval mastery*, pp. 48-54.
[21] Roberts, Roberts, and Bisson, *History of England*, chapter 14; J. I. Israel, 'The emerging empire: The continental perspective, 1650-1713', in The Oxford History of the British Empire: Volume 1, the origins of the empire, British overseas enterprise to the close of the seventeenth century, ed. by N. Canny, 5 vols (Oxford: Oxford University Press, 1998), pp. 423-444, (p. 423); Kennedy, *British naval mastery*, p. 54.
[22] Roberts, Roberts, and Bisson, *History of England*, chapter 14.
[23] Jones, Anglo-Dutch Wars, introduction.

[24] Ormrod and Rommelse, 'Introduction', p. 20.
[25] Gaunt, The English Civil War, p. 246.
[26] Israel, 'The emerging empire', pp. 426-27.
[27] Gaunt, The English Civil War, p. 246; Kennedy, British naval mastery, p. 55.
[28] Roberts, Roberts, and Bisson, History of England, chapter 14.
[29] Roberts, Roberts, and Bisson, History of England, chapter 14; Kennedy, British naval mastery, p. 57.
[30] Gaunt, The English Civil War, pp. 248-49; Kennedy, British naval mastery, p. 58.
[31] Kennedy, British naval mastery, p. 58.
[32] Jones, Anglo-Dutch Wars, introduction.
[33] Kennedy, British naval mastery, p. 60.
[34] Rodger, Command of the ocean, p. 95.
[35] Kennedy, British naval mastery, p. 65; Rodger, Command of the ocean, p. 183.
[36] Rodger, Command of the ocean, p. 80.
[37] Kennedy, British naval mastery, p. 66.
[38] Jones, Anglo-Dutch Wars, introduction.
[39] Schama, The British Wars, chapter 4, discusses this problem.
[40] J. Miller, The Glorious Revolution, 2nd edition (Abingdon: Routledge, 2014), chapter 1.
[41] B. Best, William of Orange and the fight for the Crown of England: The Glorious Revolution (Barnsley: Frontline Books, 2021), chapter 12; Miller, The Glorious Revolution, chapter 1.
[42] Best, William of Orange, chapter 12; Miller, The Glorious Revolution, chapter 1.
[43] Miller, The Glorious Revolution, chapter 1; M. I. Wilson, Happy and glorious: The revolution of 1688 (Stroud: The History Press, 2014), chapter 5.
[44] Wilson, Happy and glorious, chapter 5.
[45] Miller, The Glorious Revolution, chapter 1.
[46] Best, William of Orange, chapter 12; Schama, The British Wars, chapter 4.
[47] Schama, The British Wars, chapter 4.
[48] Best, William of Orange, chapter 12.
[49] Best, William of Orange, chapter 12; Roberts, Roberts and Bisson, History of England, chapter 15.
[50] Schama, The British Wars, chapter 4.
[51] Gaunt, The English Civil War, pp. 249-51; Kennedy, British naval mastery, p. 65; Schama, The British Wars, chapter 4.
[52] Israel, 'The emerging empire', p. 441.
[53] Gaunt, The English Civil War, pp. 248-49; Schama, The British Wars, chapter 4.
[54] Kennedy, British naval mastery, pp. 65-66.
[55] Kennedy, British naval mastery, pp. 62-65; Ormrod and Rommelse, 'Introduction', pp. 10-11.

[56] D. Armitage, *The ideological origins of the British Empire*, (Cambridge: Cambridge University Press, 2000), p. 101.
[57] Darwin, *Unfinished empire*, p. xi; R. Tombs, *The English and their history*, (London: Allen Lane, 2014), pp. 275-76.
[58] Israel, 'The emerging empire', p. 441; Kennedy, *British naval mastery*, p. 63.
[59] Darwin, *Unfinished empire*, p. 10.
[60] Kennedy, *British naval mastery*, p. 60.

Chapter 9: The Global Situation

Section 1: Introduction and Explanations

Finally, it's time to end our exploration of the early British Empire by discussing how far Britain had come by the early eighteenth century. We've studied a lot of themes and discussed many important events, but how much difference did these really make? Was Britain now a global power with an empire, ready to rule the world?

To answer this question, we naturally need to know what was happening in the rest of the world. We discussed this a little when we looked at the Mughal and Ottoman Empires, so it may be a good idea to revisit those if your memories about them have faded. However, there is one crucial country that we haven't looked at in-depth yet. China. Thus, one of the explanations here focuses on China's Qing dynasty.

The other explanation breaks down an idea you may not be familiar with, but which is vital to understanding the developments of this period. Proto-industrialisation.

What was the Qing dynasty?

The Qing dynasty was China's last imperial dynasty and ruled from 1644-1911. Its rulers were not actually ethnic Chinese. They were Manchus who took advantage of the chaos and rebellions of the final years of the Ming dynasty, working with Chinese collaborators to seize power.

The Manchu conquest was swift and brutal. Massacres were commonplace, and the Chinese people suffered all manner of abuses and humiliations. The conquerors gave all Chinese men ten days to adopt the traditional Manchu hairstyle of a long pigtail and shaved head. If they refused to do so, their new overlords executed them.

Furthermore, for the first century or so of their reign, the Manchus hoarded all political power for themselves. However, later in the eighteenth century, they allowed some ethnic Chinese citizens to rise in the civil service as the Kangxi emperor began integrating the ruling regime more closely into Chinese culture. Despite this, large portions of the population always saw the Qing dynasty as a foreign invader.

Although the initial conquest was brutal, the Qing were, at first, decent rulers. They provided secure and stable government in the eighteenth century, allowing cities to flourish and businesses to prosper. The population rose, and manufacturing increased. China even opened up to long-distance and global trade for a time. However, beneath this appearance of success, the seeds for destruction were already being sown.

At the start of the nineteenth century, the Qing dynasty was undeniably wealthy. Still, the empire was expensive to maintain. The expansionist policies of the Qianlong emperor, ruling from 1735-1796, resulted in several wars, high spending, and a large and costly standing army.

The success of the Qing rulers also made them resistant to change, which left them unable to keep up with the rising European powers. This was especially true after Qianlong reversed the open trade policies of his predecessors. Ultimately, this resistance cost them dearly.

Throughout the nineteenth century, external invasions (like the Opium Wars) and internal revolts (like the widespread and bloody Taiping Rebellion) weakened the authority of the Qing government. Foreign powers on Chinese soil acted virtually however they wanted, and the population, unsurprisingly, grew resentful. It didn't help that living conditions were terrible for many people, especially rural peasants.

These issues culminated in the Boxer Uprising, where some Chinese men believed they had mystical powers which they could use to repel the foreign invaders. Foolishly, the Dowager Empress Cixi (a controversial and unpopular figure) decided to side with the Boxers against the foreign powers.

The Qing dynasty was humiliated once again as they faced the West's overwhelming firepower. The Western powers forced the Qing to make even more concessions, although they still resisted in small ways, such as refusing to allow girls to be educated (leaving this in the hands of private benefactors).

Eventually, the troubles of the Qing dynasty grew too much for the people of China to bear. A coalition of many different groups rose up and overthrew the government. Sadly, this did not lead to peace and stability for China. Initially, a network of local warlords seized control of the country before the nationalist Kuomintang (KMT) and the Chinese Communist Party joined forces to establish a national government. Shortly after this, the KMT betrayed and massacred many communists and established a one-party dictatorship.[1]

What is proto-industrialisation?

You probably already know what industrialisation is. Put simply, it's the process of becoming more industrial, which basically means producing more manufactured goods. We often think of this in terms of the massive machines of the industrial revolution. But in that case, what is proto-industrialisation?

The Collins dictionary defines 'proto' as 'primitive, ancestral, or original: prototype'. In short, proto-industrialisation is the early stage of the development of industry. This term often refers to small cottage industries or handicrafts that produce goods to sell. This could be the relatively small scale, possibly rural, production of various goods such as soap, glass, lace, and weavings which often involved women and children.[2]

Section 2: Britain's Place in the World by the Early Eighteenth Century

The last two chapters showed that by the early eighteenth century, Britain was beginning to take a form that we would recognise today and developing expertise to help it forge a global empire. In this chapter, I want to look at Britain's place in the world by this time and show that the conditions were ready for Britain to take its young empire to another level.

The growth of the American colonies

By the early eighteenth century, Britain's land in North America had grown substantially from the early colonies that we discussed in chapter six. They had founded Pennsylvania, expanded into the site of the future Carolinas, and taken New York from the Dutch.[3]

Likewise, many more Britons had emigrated to the American colonies, and the British population of North America had reached around 265,000.[4] This population growth proved to be a distinct advantage to the British in their many conflicts with France during the coming century, as the two nations repeatedly clashed over the continent.[5]

However, although Britain's population and landholding in America left them primed for success, they still had a long way to go. For example, by 1770, the population of Britain's mainland colonies had reached around 2.3 million. Likewise, although the British West Indies had a substantial population of 145,000 in the early eighteenth century, by 1815, it had risen to 877,000.[6] The colonies had grown, but they were still comparatively small compared to their later selves.

The British colonies were also becoming increasingly tied to the state. The government made efforts to achieve this throughout the late seventeenth century, with things reaching a climax during the reign of James II.[7] Many colonists were quite resentful of James' policies and sided with William of Orange during the Glorious Revolution.[8]

There has been some disagreement over whether the colonists benefitted from this arrangement. Generally, it seems that they were able to remove James' harsher, more oppressive policies and have some of their liberties restored.[9] However, many of James' centralising policies continued, and the Glorious Revolution's ultimate effect was to assert royal dominance in the American colonies.[10] This was especially true in the West Indies, where the nature of the sugar trade meant that the colonists required closer ties to the throne to protect their interests. Control on the mainland remained a little looser.[11]

As of yet, these closer ties were not a cause for significant tension; with James and his unpopular policies gone, many people welcomed them.[12] However, this rosy state of affairs didn't last forever. Over time the increasing royal involvement in the colonies became the subject of many political debates. It profoundly impacted the empire's development across the eighteenth century and culminated in the American Revolution.[13]

The American colonies were also becoming more economically similar to how they would look in the later eighteenth century. The colonists had finally abandoned their search for gold and now focused on commerce and agriculture.[14]

Likewise, British America was finally becoming one united whole. The founding (or capture) of new ports like Philadelphia and New York helped connect the formerly isolated colonies.[15] These ports also managed trade for a vast commercial network across America, rather than simply serving their local areas, which further helped to unify the colonies.[16]

In the Caribbean, the economy was also taking a significant new shape that would define its future. Sugar production increased throughout the seventeenth century. Unfortunately, the work was harsh and unpopular. This led plantation owners to turn to slavery in order to fill their workforce, meaning that by 1715 the black population in the British Caribbean far outstripped the white.[17]

Of course, many colonies still looked nothing like what they would become. In the early eighteenth century, the Carolinas were relatively equal societies (compared to England) with limited slaveholding. This changed significantly, and the Carolinas soon became prominent slave states.[18]

Nevertheless, although the British Empire in America would naturally still change and grow, by the beginning of the eighteenth century, it had taken on a form that most students of the empire would recognise. The foundations had been laid for many of the dramatic political, military, and economic events of the eighteenth century. The British state now controlled a relatively centralised and increasingly commercial network across the Atlantic. In short, the formal British Empire had taken shape in the Americas.

Limits in Africa and Asia

However, the expansion of formal control was at this time still limited to the Americas as most emigrants from England in the seventeenth century had gone to Ireland or America.[19] As John Darwin said, although there were 'distinctively British communities' in America, British communities in Asia often numbered only in the dozens or very rarely in the hundreds.[20] British holdings in Asia at this time were purely commercial; they were essentially factories and trading posts that naturally had minimal populations.[21]

The picture was very similar in Africa. British holdings there were primarily small forts, factories, and trading posts.[22] Attempts at creating any plantations had been small-scale and ultimately unsuccessful.[23] The English presence was limited to the coast and less significant than the Dutch and Portuguese. West Africa was also not a substantial market for English exports.[24]

England had very little political influence. Their forts were primarily there to protect trade from other Europeans, not to assert influence over indigenous leaders. Even in the early eighteenth century, African rulers held power over British leaders, with one expelling them from their fort at Ouidah.[25] So, despite Britain having made significant steps towards creating a formal empire in the Americas, their holdings in Africa and Asia were still minimal and commercial as opposed to colonial.

European limitations

The British were not alone in having limited global influence by the early eighteenth century. Although the Spanish, Portuguese, and Dutch had a head start on Britain, the world's great powers were still found in Asia and not in Europe. However, it should be noted that signs that this situation could soon change had started to appear.

European power rose after the Portuguese began their explorations, and Columbus discovered the Americas for Spain in the late fifteenth century.[26] This increased the strength of European nations and weakened Asian empires as Europe was now taking on the significant trading role that had previously belonged to Central Asian and Middle Eastern powers.[27]

For example, the Ottoman Empire was a dangerous threat to Europe in the sixteenth century. It took advantage of European divisions to seize critical locations, threatening the Mediterranean and Central Europe.[28] However, by the end of the century, it was in decline. It is unlikely to be a coincidence that this happened at the same time as disruption to their economy because of gold and silver flowing out from the Americas.[29]

Clearly, the growth of European power was well underway, but it was still in its relatively early stages. Far Eastern countries still outclassed European nations by some margin. India had been the world's largest economy until, in around 1500, China overtook it.[30] China would not lose its place as the strongest economy in the world until the turn of the nineteenth century.[31] In fact, it was not clear at the time that it would ever do so. The rulers of Qing dynasty China remained politically strong enough to decide when to allow Europeans to trade in their country throughout the seventeenth and eighteenth centuries.[32] Many of the economic developments occurring within Europe at this time were also happening in China. Kenneth Pomeranz goes so far as to argue that had Europe not had access to so many overseas resources (the Americas), it may not ever have overtaken China's economic power to the degree it did.[33] In short, Europe as a whole was not yet dominant at the dawn of the eighteenth century, even if it was growing stronger all the time.

Imperial developments within Britain

Developments based in Britain itself were also changing the country's place in the world.

Naval power

England's increasing naval strength, shown by its victory in the First Anglo-Dutch War (1652-54), was an early sign of its imperial potential.[34] By the end of the seventeenth century, the size of the English fleet began to outstrip the French.[35] Following the Glorious Revolution, this naval growth, combined with England's alliance with the Dutch and Scots, severely weakened France's global position.[36]

Alongside this military growth, England's civilian maritime future also looked to be heading in the right direction.

By the late seventeenth century, the English were becoming the dominant power in long-distance and colonial shipping (although the Dutch were still more important in trade within Europe).[37]

Despite these advances, newly formed Britain's power was precarious at the start of the eighteenth century. For instance, shipping was still vulnerable to French attacks, and British imperial strength remained very reliant on the alliance with the Dutch.[38] Nevertheless, by the end of the War of Spanish Succession (1707-1714), Britain had been confirmed as Europe's dominant maritime and colonial power.[39]

Population Growth and industry

A vast population explosion began in Britain in 1696, which naturally contributed to the economy and the state's power in many ways as it provided both workers and consumers.[40] Likewise, throughout the seventeenth century, England had gradually become more urbanised and industrialised than its European neighbours, beginning with a process of 'proto industrialisation.'[41]

However, Britain remained far from the industrial metropolis of the Victorian age that dominates popular perceptions of the British Empire. By 1700, only 13% of people lived in towns with a population greater than 10,000.[42] Likewise, most of the country's wealth was still based on agriculture.[43] Thus, although Britain was on the verge of a population boom, urbanisation was still in its very early stages.

Sugar and slavery

The early eighteenth century was a time of growth for British merchants, especially those involved in two particular trades. The first of these was sugar. British sugar producers took over more and more of the market as they gained the upper hand in a price war with their Brazil-based Portuguese competitors.[44] Sugar became cheaper, and its consumption rose rapidly.[45] The future of British sugar planters looked bright indeed. Unfortunately, there was a darker side to this economic boom.

Along with a rise in sugar production came an increase in slavery. By 1700, enslaved people had become West Africa's most valuable export.[46] These people weren't all destined for the Caribbean, of course. Slavery was also rising in mainland America.[47] However, slavery was particularly critical to the development of the Caribbean colonies as free workers would simply not accept the horrendous working conditions on sugar plantations. It didn't take long for the population to reflect this.[48] By the early eighteenth century, the sugar and slaving industries that would be so crucial in the expansion of the British Empire were already well established.

Reforms in Trade

Commerce, in general, had grown in the seventeenth century, and its nature had changed.[49] Englishmen gradually became more directly involved, while trade with Asia (especially India) became increasingly important.[50]

Similarly, trade became more open. The Crown had previously granted monopolies to individuals or groups, allowing them to dominate a particular industry; however, fewer of these were renewed after the Glorious Revolution.[51] This relaxation of official controls allowed more people to seek their fortunes in global trade.[52] Likewise, the East India Company had been forced to reform, allowing opportunities for a broader range of people to become involved with the Company.[53]

In short, the legal and commercial characteristics of the later British Empire were becoming more fully formed.

Changes in government

The multiple regime changes of the seventeenth century led to various reforms that contributed to growth in

Britain's economic power and imperial potential. For instance, the privatisation of land and mineral rights after the restoration of Charles II made many merchants and investors much wealthier.[54] The government also became much more involved in actions overseas throughout the seventeenth century.[55]

Following 1688, these changes began to accelerate. Tax revenues rose, a trend that would continue across the century. Furthermore, kings and ministers could no longer ignore the demands of parliament and the House of Commons.[56] This is particularly interesting, as the makeup of parliament also changed at this time. Although wealthy landowners still dominated the seats, there was now a large group whose interests were rooted primarily in the colonies.[57] They would therefore pressure the leaders of Britain to pay more attention to global and imperial affairs.

It would be wrong to say that Britain now focussed entirely on its colonies. Giving William III, a Dutch king, the throne also tied Britain deeper into European conflicts.[58] In its own way, this also contributed to the growth of Britain's empire. Britain remained committed to maintaining a balance of power in Europe. This is unsurprising as much of Britain's trade at this time was still with the continent.[59] Brendan Simms even argues that Britain built its empire because of its involvement in Europe and the many diplomatic tangles that came with it.[60]

Nevertheless, whether Britain's eyes were on Europe or the wider world, political changes were undoubtedly beginning to alter the character of Britain's government.

Britain was ready to cement an empire

Overall, although the British Empire was still a long way from what it would become under the Victorians, many of the pre-requisites for its future global dominance were already in place in the early eighteenth century.

[1] Sources:
Bickers, R., *The scramble for China: Foreign devils in the Qing Empire, 1832-1914* (London: Penguin, 2012).
Fenby, J., *The Penguin history of modern China: The fall and rise of a great power, 1850 to the present*, 3rd edition (London: penguin, 2019).
Frankopan, P., *The silk roads: A new history of the world*, paperback edition (London: Bloomsbury, 2016).
Kerr. H., *A short history of China: From ancient dynasties to economic powerhouse* (Harpenden: Pocket Essentials, 2013).
McMahon, D., *Rethinking the decline of China's Qing dynasty: Imperial activism and borderland management at the turn of the nineteenth century* (Abingdon: Routledge, 2014).
Pletcher, K., *The History of China* (New York: Britannica Educational Publishing, 2011).
Rowe, W. T., *China's last empire: The Great Qing*, paperback edition (London: Harvard University Press, 2012).
Smith, R. J., *The Qing dynasty and traditional Chinese culture* (London: Rowman and Littlefield, 2015).
Wood, M., *The story of China: A Portrait of a civilisation and its people* (London: Simon and Schuster, 2020).

[2] Sources:
Collins English Dictionary, 13th edition (Glasgow: Collins, 2018).
Cipolla, C. M., *Before the Industrial Revolution: European society and economy, 1000-1700*, 3rd edition (London: Routledge 1993).
Mokyr, J. 'Editor's introduction: The new economic history and the Industrial Revolution', in *The British Industrial Revolution: An economic perspective*, ed. by J. Mokyr, Routledge edition (Abingdon: Routledge 2018).
Pomeranz, K. *The Great Divergence: China, Europe, and the making of the modern world economy*, (Princeton: Princeton University Press, 2000).
Schama, S., *A history of Britain: At the edge of the world? 3000BC-AD1603*, Kindle edition (London: Bodley Head, 2009).

[3] P. J. Marshall, 'Introduction' in *The Oxford History of the British Empire: Volume 2, The eighteenth century*, ed. by P. J. Marshall, 5 vols (Oxford: Oxford University Press, 1998), pp. 1-26, (p. 2).
[4] J. Black, *The British Empire: A history and a debate*, (London: Routledge, 2015), chapter 2; Marshall, 'Introduction', p. 2.
[5] Black, *The British Empire*, chapter 2.
[6] Marshall, 'Introduction', p. 2.
[7] H. McD. Beckles, 'The "Hub of Empire": The Caribbean and Britain in the seventeenth century', in *The Oxford History of the British Empire: Volume 1, the origins of the empire, British overseas enterprise to the close of the seventeenth*

century, ed. by N. Canny, 5 vols (Oxford: Oxford University Press, 1998), pp. 218-240, (p. 236); N. Dalziel, *The Penguin historical atlas of the British Empire* (London: Penguin, 2006), p. 28.

[8] Dalziel, *Historical atlas*, p. 28; R. S. Dunn, 'The Glorious Revolution and America', in *The Oxford History of the British Empire: Volume 1, the origins of the empire, British overseas enterprise to the close of the seventeenth century*, ed. by N. Canny, 5 vols (Oxford: Oxford University Press, 1998), pp. 445-465, (p. 446).

[9] Dalziel, *Historical atlas*, p. 28; Dunn, 'Glorious Revolution and America', p. 446.

[10] D. S. Lovejoy, *The Glorious Revolution in America*, Wesleyan edition, (Hanover: Wesleyan University Press, 1987), pp. 377-78.

[11] Dunn, 'Glorious Revolution and America', p. 465.

[12] Dunn, 'Glorious Revolution and America', p. 446.

[13] G. Chet, *The colonists' American Revolution: Preserving English liberty, 1607-1783* (Hoboken: Wiley Blackwell, 2020), pp. 79-96; F. O'Gorman, *The long eighteenth century: British political and social history, 1688-1832*, 2nd edition (London: Bloomsbury, 2016), pp. 199-206; J. Shy, 'The American colonies in war and revolution, 1748-1783', in *The Oxford History of the British Empire: Volume 2, The eighteenth century*, ed. by P. J. Marshall, 5 vols (Oxford: Oxford University Press, 1998), pp. 300-324; B. Tuchman, *The march of folly: From Troy to Vietnam*, Abacus edition (London: Abacus, 1990), pp. 155-288.

[14] A. Pagden, 'The struggle for legitimacy and the image of empire in the Atlantic to c.1700', in *The Oxford History of the British Empire: Volume 1, the origins of the empire, British overseas enterprise to the close of the seventeenth century*, ed. by N. Canny, 5 vols (Oxford: Oxford University Press, 1998), pp. 34-54, (p. 36).

[15] N. C. Landsman, 'The middle colonies: New opportunities for settlement, 1660-1700', in *The Oxford History of the British Empire: Volume 1, the origins of the empire, British overseas enterprise to the close of the seventeenth century*, ed. by N. Canny, 5 vols (Oxford: Oxford University Press, 1998), pp. 351-373, (pp. 372-73).

[16] Landsman, 'The middle colonies', pp. 372-73.

[17] Beckles, 'Hub of empire', pp. 223-226.

[18] R. M. Weir, '"Shaftesbury's darling": British settlement in the Carolinas and the Close of the seventeenth century', in *The Oxford History of the British Empire: Volume 1, the origins of the empire, British overseas enterprise to the close of the seventeenth century*, ed. by N. Canny, 5 vols (Oxford: Oxford University Press, 1998), pp. 375-397, (pp. 394-95).

[19] J. Horn, 'Tobacco colonies: the shaping of English society in the Seventeenth-Century Chesapeake in *The Oxford History of the British Empire: Volume 1, the origins of the empire, British overseas enterprise to the close of the*

seventeenth century, ed. by N. Canny, 5 vols (Oxford: Oxford University Press, 1998), pp. 170-192, (p. 30).

[20] J. Darwin, *Unfinished empire: The global expansion of Britain*, Penguin edition (London: Penguin, 2013), p. 50.

[21] Horn, 'Tobacco colonies', pp. 28-29; Marshall, 'Introduction', p. 2.

[22] P. E. H. Hair, and R. Law, 'The English in Western Africa to 1700', in *The Oxford History of the British Empire: Volume 1, the origins of the empire, British overseas enterprise to the close of the seventeenth century*, ed. by N. Canny, 5 vols (Oxford: Oxford University Press, 1998), pp. 241-262, (pp. 260-61); Horn, 'Tobacco colonies', pp. 28-29.

[23] Hair and Law, 'Western Africa', pp. 260-61.

[24] Darwin, *Unfinished empire*, pp. 42-43; Hair and Law, 'Western Africa', pp. 260-62.

[25] Darwin, *Unfinished empire*, p. 43.

[26] J. Darwin, *After Tamerlane: The rise and fall of global empires, 1400-2000*, Penguin edition (London: Penguin, 2008), pp. 51-56; P. Frankopan, *The silk roads: A new history of the world*, paperback edition (London: Bloomsbury, 2016), pp. xviii, 202-06; J. M. Roberts and O. A. Westad, *The Penguin history of the world*, 6th edition (London: Penguin, 2013), pp. 521-522.

[27] Frankopan, *The silk roads*, pp. xiv-xviii, 202-06.

[28] H. Inalcik, *The Ottoman Empire: The classical age, 1300-1600*, ebook edition (London: Orion Books, 2013), chapter 5.

[29] Frankopan, *The silk roads*, p. 239; Inalcik, *Ottoman Empire*, chapter 6.

[30] M., Wood, *The story of India*, Kindle edition (London: BBC Books, 2008).

[31] K. Pomeranz, *The Great Divergence: China, Europe, and the making of the modern world economy*, (Princeton: Princeton University Press, 2000); M., Wood, *The story of China: A Portrait of a civilisation and its people* (London: Simon and Schuster, 2020), p. 341.

[32] R. Bickers, *The scramble for China: Foreign devils in the Qing Empire, 1832-1914* (London: Penguin, 2012), p. 18; Frankopan, *The silk roads*, p. 270.

[33] Pomeranz, *Great Divergence*, introduction.

[34] J. I. Israel, 'The emerging empire: The continental perspective, 1650-1713', in *The Oxford History of the British Empire: Volume 1, the origins of the empire, British overseas enterprise to the close of the seventeenth century*, ed. by N. Canny, 5 vols (Oxford: Oxford University Press, 1998), pp. 423-444, (p. 423).

[35] G. E. Alymer, 'Navy, state, trade and empire', in *The Oxford History of the British Empire: Volume 1, the origins of the empire, British overseas enterprise to the close of the seventeenth century*, ed. by N. Canny, 5 vols (Oxford: Oxford University Press, 1998), pp. 467-480, (p. 473).

[36] Israel, 'The emerging empire', p. 443-44.

[37] J. M. Price, 'The Imperial economy 1700-1776', in *The Oxford History of the British Empire: Volume 2, The eighteenth century*, ed. by P. J. Marshall, 5 vols (Oxford: Oxford University Press, 1998), pp. 78-104, (p. 79).
[38] Alymer, 'Navy, state, trade', p. 473; Israel, 'The emerging empire', pp. 441-42.
[39] Black, *The British Empire*, chapter 2; Israel, 'The emerging empire', pp. 443-44.
[40] Price, 'Imperial economy', p. 79.
[41] P. K. O'Brien, 'Inseparable connections: Trade, economy, fiscal state, and the expansion of empire, 1688-1815', in *The Oxford History of the British Empire: Volume 2, The eighteenth century*, ed. by P. J. Marshall, 5 vols (Oxford: Oxford University Press, 1998), pp. 53-77, (p. 56).
[42] O'Gorman, *Long eighteenth century*, p. 24.
[43] O'Gorman, *Long eighteenth century*, p. 25.
[44] James, *Rise and fall*, p. 17.
[45] N. Zahedieh, 'Overseas expansion and trade in the seventeenth century', in *The Oxford History of the British Empire: Volume 1, the origins of the empire, British overseas enterprise to the close of the seventeenth century*, ed. by N. Canny, 5 vols (Oxford: Oxford University Press, 1998), pp. 398-421, (p. 410).
[46] Dalziel, *Historical atlas*, p. 30.
[47] Dalziel, *Historical atlas*, p. 16.
[48] Beckles, 'Hub of empire', p. 227.
[49] Zahedieh, 'Overseas expansion', p. 399; O'Brien, 'Inseparable connections', p. 53.
[50] P. J. Marshall, 'The English in Asia to 1700', in *The Oxford History of the British Empire: Volume 1, the origins of the empire, British overseas enterprise to the close of the seventeenth century*, ed. by N. Canny, 5 vols (Oxford: Oxford University Press, 1998), pp. 264-285, (pp. 283-84); Zahedieh, 'Overseas expansion', p. 399.
[51] O'Brien, 'Inseparable connections', p. 60.
[52] Zahedieh, 'Overseas expansion', p. 403.
[53] Marshall, 'English in Asia', pp. 282-83.
[54] O'Brien, 'Inseparable connections', p. 57.
[55] M. J. Braddick, 'The English government, war, trade and settlement, 1625-1688', in *The Oxford History of the British Empire: Volume 1, the origins of the empire, British overseas enterprise to the close of the seventeenth century*, ed. by N. Canny, 5 vols (Oxford: Oxford University Press, 1998), pp. 287-308, p. 307.
[56] L. James, *The rise and fall of the British Empire*, new edition (London: Abacus, 1998), pp. 52-53.
[57] James, *Rise and fall*, pp. 52-53.
[58] O'Gorman, *Long eighteenth century*, pp. 56-57.

[59] B. Simms, *Three victories and a defeat: The rise and fall of the First British Empire, 1714-1783*, Penguin edition (London: Penguin, 2008), pp. 45, 74.
[60] Simms, *Three victories*, pp. 75-76.

You made it!

Congratulations on finishing this book! I hope that you enjoyed the journey and learned a few things on the way. If you did, then please consider leaving a review. They are so, so important in helping my books to reach more people and helping me to keep writing.

About the author

Daniel Allen has loved history for as long as he can remember. This started with watching historical films and reading historical fiction and soon progressed into more serious study.

He holds a BA in History and Ancient History and an MA in History, specialising in imperial and global history, both from the University of Exeter. This let him study a huge range of topics, from Ancient Greece and Persia to the Cold War.

Now he aims to share his love of history with others by publishing accessible and affordable books.

Printed in Great Britain
by Amazon